Marriage
Is a Loving Business

Le Nelson   April-87

Marriage Is a Loving Business

Paul A. Hauck

The Westminster Press
Philadelphia

Published by The Westminster Press ®
Philadelphia, Pennsylvania

Printed in the United States of America

4   5   6   7   8   9

Library of Congress Cataloging in Publication Data

Hauck, Paul A
  Marriage is a loving business.

  Bibliography: p.
  1. Marriage. 2. Marriage counseling. I. Title.
HQ734.H384   362.8'2   77–2202
ISBN 0–664–24137–9

*For Kathy and Henry's delightful
and quite unique Teresa*

Contents

Preface

Last year there were over one million divorces in America. For each couple who divorced we can be certain that many other couples were thinking of divorce or were leading unhappy married lives.

Marriage is, without question, one of the most enduring and one of the most important of all social institutions. People who have done poorly at a half dozen marriages don't flinch about walking down the aisle a seventh time, so powerful is the attraction to the comforts of mating. One young man said to me on the threshold of my office door, just before going to see his divorce lawyer at the end of the hall, "Well, maybe I'll have better luck next time."

Most people do not think of remarrying that soon. They need time to recover. However, they do recover and they often remarry also.

After working as a psychotherapist for over two decades I realized that most people (professionals included) have no clear idea of what love and marriage are intrinsically all about. The more I puzzled over the nature of the difficulties that couples were having with each other, the more I began to see an explanation for love and marriage that finally made sense to me. Until then I was puzzled as to how to help married people. Secretly I wished that the next client coming in the office would have a straightforward neurotic problem with which I was comfortable, rather than a marital problem which I felt at a loss to deal with.

My difficulty with marriage counseling stemmed from not having a theory of love and marriage that helped me realize what was happening. So I decided to think up explanations to account for healthy and unhealthy marriages. Suddenly I began to look forward to marriage counseling. What I started out fearing, I ended up welcoming.

In the following pages I offer my theory of love and marriage. I warn you, however, I am a realist. I do not especially like all the conclusions at which I have arrived. Indeed, I truly wish my theories sounded more romantic and more flattering to human nature. On the contrary, some of my conclusions are a bit raw, objective, and cold. I can't help that. If you keep an open mind about my views and check them carefully against your own experiences, I think you'll come to the same conclusions I did. When you see your most important relationships in the terms I've used to describe them in this book, you will know why you do what you do with respect to your mate. And whether you take a firm stand or give in, my theory of love and marriage will be a guide and comfort in helping you decide which decisions to make.

Do not be misled into thinking that this knowledge will automatically help your marriage. I surely suspect it will do that in a great many instances. However, a proper understanding of this book, properly applied, will almost certainly encourage some couples into periods of dispute for varying lengths of time, and others into outright separation or divorce.

This, too, I cannot help. Some marriages are such colossal mistakes that they can only be cured by termination.

Lastly, for those interested in seeking help for their marriages, I have devoted a chapter to the marriage counselor, one of the most skilled of all psychotherapists. I do this in the hope that those persons who have troubled marriages will not delay seeking the help that could make a world of difference to them, in many cases in a short period of time.

If this book accomplishes this last goal and no other, I will feel most gratified.

P.A.H.

Chapter 1
The Mythology
of Marriage

Iwant you to read parts of a letter I received this year. It is pathetic but not unlike others I have had before. To protect the sender, I have removed all identifying information. No matter. The gist of her message is what counts and is almost enough to make me angry at her husband, and at her too.

Dear Dr. Hauck:

I mentioned to my husband this morning I was planning on joining a bowling league with a few of my girl friends. He had a fit. Said I don't deserve a night out and that I'm using bowling as an excuse to get out. You see, Dr. Hauck, he thinks I'm a tramp because I got drunk once and came home after eleven.

Ever since that night I've gone through hell with him asking questions after questions on who did I talk to, etc., etc.

I'm plenty upset over this because my husband is a drunk and has had many affairs. He's often home when the sun comes up. But that's different.

I want to go to work, not only to save my sanity, but to buy things I've never had. In the many years we've been married I've never had a new stove and other things. I want to fix up my house because he just doesn't care. If it were up to him, we'd rent all the time. You should see some of the dumps he's put me in. But to him my wanting to work for nice things is just another reason to run around.

Once I worked in a factory and the only way to keep the pressure of my husband off me was to agree that I'd save all my money so we could build a house. He even promised to pay my gas money and give me extra to buy lunches. Of course, he never did. The money

I had saved I spent bailing him out of jail for drinking.
My sister is going through the same mess I am. She couldn't join
clubs or have friends either. That scares me. I have such pent-up and
mixed-up feelings of hate that I feel guilty over them.

There's more, but surely you get the picture. Her basic problem is that she hasn't the foggiest idea of what marriage is all about. Does she believe in a double standard, one for her husband, one for herself? Of course she does. Does she think of herself as an inferior member of her marriage? That's obvious. Would she tolerate such abuse if she were treated this way in her job? Not on your life. She doesn't realize that her marriage is as much of a business as her job. Had she this insight, the story of her marriage might not have been so sad.

The lives of millions of men and women would improve greatly if they saw their marriages as actual business deals entitling them to certain privileges for which they now plead. Instead of feeling guilty over claiming their rights, men and women would do so as easily in marriage as they now do on their jobs. To understand this point of view, we must first understand something about love.

WHAT IS THIS THING CALLED LOVE?

Years ago, while giving a talk to a community group, I was asked by a woman in the audience what love is. I thought the question foolish and put her off with such dodges as: "You know what love is. It's a strong emotional tie between two persons who feel close, miss each other, and want only good for the loved one."

This was double-talk and left us both dissatisfied. The question bothered me for years until I arrived at a definition of love that made sense. I confess it sounds cold and unfeeling, judging by the reactions of those to whom I have explained it. Nevertheless, I'm sticking to it because it squares with my observations in and out of clinical practice.

Love is the feeling you have for someone who satisfies, has satisfied, or will satisfy your needs and deepest desires.

It doesn't sound profound, does it? Perhaps you haven't noticed the total meaning of the statement. It means that you love people *because* they are good to you, *because* they please you, *because* you're important to them. And if they don't please you, you tend not to love them. If they reject you, you are likely to reject them.

This means that you love people *only* for what you think they *will* do, *are* doing, or *have* done for you. First you love the doing and then love the person *because* he or she performs those kind and satisfying acts. *You never love anyone just because of themselves.* ? This view is totally contrary to the popular notion put forth by romantic writers and poets.

To further establish this rather practical view of love, consider the following:

1. A divorce always means that two persons are frustrated with each other. The complaints in a divorce action always involve such things as cruelty, unfaithfulness, and incompatibility. In other words one mate is not giving the other those satisfactions and fulfilling those needs which brought them together. So they fall out of love for exactly those reasons.

2. Marriage counseling almost always involves one party complaining about the objectionable behavior of the other. In over two decades as a psychotherapist I have never talked to a couple who were satisfying each other in all major respects but were getting a divorce anyway. On the contrary, there are always one or more powerful complaints from one or both parties. This observation has led me to ask early in a marriage counseling interview for each person to tell me outright how he or she is being frustrated by the mate. It is the frustration, the disappointment in having one's needs and desires unsatisfied, that causes them to fall *out* of love. They certainly aren't frustrated because they are being completely fulfilled.

3. We fall in love with that person whom we think can satisfy our needs and desires best, or whom we think is the best we can get.

Louise wanted to feel important to someone and she wanted security, a handsome mate, and someone on whom she could lean. The ideal mate for this combination of wishes would be a fellow who *(a)* wanted her greatly (she would then feel important), *(b)*

13

was wealthy (for her security), *(c)* a movie star (for his body and looks), and *(d)* a general (he would be of strong character and not afraid to make decisions).

The likelihood of finding one man with all these qualities was very poor. So she compromised and married the man who came closest to her ideal, *and* who asked her to marry him. He was devoted to her for several years but later showed dwindling attention. He started out earning good money but wasn't getting raises to keep up with the expenses of raising three children. He was lean and athletic when they married but he gradually lost his shape because of little exercise and too much beer before the television set each night. As she saw these requirements for happiness fade slowly one by one she also lost confidence in his counsel. That, added to the other disappointments, caused the most natural thing to happen to her feelings of love—they began to diminish. What was there to love him for? His money, looks, decision-making, and attention were not being delivered. So she fell out of love. And why shouldn't she? If she couldn't get acceptable and important behavior out of him, how was he different from any stranger who would give her as little?

This didn't mean that she had to hate him. She could disapprove of his actions and still not damn him as a person. But, love him? Hardly! We reserve that feeling for those rare people who treat us special.

4. That overall, powerful feeling of love is seldom given to someone solely on the basis of one quality, such as intelligence, looks, or wealth. If you love a woman just for her body, you've got to be powerfully frustrated or immature, or both. Love wants more than one gift on which to survive. That's why we sensibly fall in love only when the loved one has a number of qualities rated highly by the lover. In addition to wanting dependability, faithfulness, beauty, and humor, or whatever, we also look for kindness, companionship, fair treatment, and the feeling of being important to that person. When these and a host of other subtle qualities are present, you fall in love. And this feeling comes *after* you convince yourself that person has these traits, *if* they are important to you.

5. What about love at first sight? True love is never based on first sight. That's possible only after you've had an opportunity to check

14

out the whole person. "First sight" love is based on one or a few qualities that draw you and interest you in that person. If your later observations prove positive, your love will grow. If not, it dies.

For example, if you see an adorable face across the room and you're smitten by Cupid, realize that your feelings are only tentative. When you begin a conversation and learn that inside that hourglass figure is an empty-sounding barrel, you've had it—if you don't like dull girls. However, if you like dull girls, you might have found a gem. It all depends on what's important to you.

6. The woman who protests that all her husband wanted her for was her body is protesting unfairly. What's wrong with wanting her body? And it's hardly likely that her looks were all that caught his admiration. She fails to realize that without her physical appeal he might not have loved her at all. Then what happens if she has an accident and loses her beauty? Am I actually suggesting that his love could die and that he might want a divorce? Precisely. I've seen it happen time and again.

If beauty and sexual satisfaction are important to a man, they form the very foundation of his love. Should his mate lose her appeal early in her marriage, there may not be enough time to develop other qualities to replace the appeal for sex. If her change in appearance occurs after thirty years of marriage, a whole lifetime of memories plus a host of other qualities can make up for the loss of sex appeal.

Rudy was married one year when he suffered brain damage on a construction job. He became irritable, forgetful, and intellectually slow. Some of the most important qualities his wife admired in him vanished overnight, and though she found it hard to admit it, so did her love. They divorced after two years.

7. "She married him for his money," they said sneeringly of Anne. Well, what's wrong with that? If money is important to you, you'll love the man or woman who has money (and it is hoped other merits as well). What's so different about your loving your mate for his many kindnesses? We could just as easily sneer at you with, "All you married him for were his kindly ways." What makes one need more valuable than another? One man's meat is another man's poison, it is said, and this applies to traits also.

Think it over and be objective about it. You've just got to

conclude that you love someone *after* you receive the kind of behavior you need and want badly. You never love anyone just because they are themselves.

8. But what about children or aged parents, neither of whom can often do a great deal for you. What can a baby do for your needs or wants? And how can an aged parent satisfy you any longer?

Children are loved despite their irritating behaviors because we *expect* them someday to act in pleasing ways. If they don't, make no mistake about it, we change our feelings of love to loathing or indifference. Parents beat and abandon their children all the time because they no longer expect their needs and desires to be satisfied by the children.

When five-year-old Roger became jealous of his baby brother and set fire to his crib and then continued setting fires all over the house despite numerous spankings, his distraught parents lost all feeling for him. My theory on love would have predicted just that.

Our parents are also not loved by us automatically. We love them because they *have been* good to us. If they had beaten, ignored, or abandoned us as children, only saints could still love them. Love must be earned.

Aged or senile parents who can no longer do us any service can still be loved because of the fond memories we have of them. We love them for what they have done and only as long as they have actually been good to us as children years before.

SUMMARY OF WHAT LOVE IS

Love grows out of a conviction that your mate will satisfy your self-interests. It is a selfish emotion based on a number of conditions that must be met first. If they are not met, the love dies, slowly or swiftly, depending on how much frustration is involved.

Do not feel guilty about falling out of love. It usually means that your needs and desires have simply not been satisfied. That was part of the problem with the lady whose letter I quoted at the beginning of this chapter. She did not understand that love, as commonly viewed, is a myth. She believed she was supposed to love her mate no matter what. Never! You love only so long as the other person is reasonably decent. Unless, of course, you happen to enjoy

16

suffering. If you think you're no good, feel guilty, and want to hang by your thumbs to do penance, a mean and selfish man will be just what the executioner ordered. And, hold on to your whip, he's going to look adorable to you precisely because he'll beat you up for nothing. So it's love again, *because* you need to be hated.

MARRIAGE ISN'T WHAT YOU THINK IT IS

I don't for a moment want to strip marriage of its wonderment, its sentiment, and the fact that it is one of the most important relationships in the lives of almost all adults all over the world. To understand it fully, however, and to see it for what it really is, you had better see marriage realistically as well as through the eyes of the poets. I have found that those people who are objective about marriage do a better job of succeeding than those who have all sorts of nonsensical notions of what wonderful things will automatically happen when they say, "I do."

Marriage is a business. It is a company of two called Mr. and Mrs. So-and-So, Inc. It requires a license from the state, a physical examination, some capital, and a place to house the company (a home). Some societies (European and Far Eastern) take marriage literally as a business arrangement. Children in India are pledged in marriage to bring powerful families together. Time was when a woman needed a cash dowry before she could consider winning a husband. In Africa a female wanting to marry felt pride in the number of cattle her father would have to pay for the honor of giving her away. If that isn't a business deal, what is?

For centuries kings and queens, princes and princesses have been marrying for political reasons, not love. If love developed later, that was fortunate but irrelevant. Marriage was a way of cementing national interests or of keeping royal blood wedded to royal blood. If that isn't business, what is?

Today we marry for business reasons also even though it may only involve the couple. The wife literally hires the man to be her husband and she expects certain services from him. He's usually expected to support her, give her his company, give her a family, take out the garbage, sweep out the garage, etc.

The man hires the woman to be a wife and will love her only

17

as long as she takes good care of the children, irons his shirts, cooks the meals, entertains his friends, or does whatever is important to him.

Whether or not the couple states this in so many words is not so important as the fact that they assume it anyway. As her employee, he is expected to do a job. And as his employee, she is expected to do hers. When either employee goofs off in this business there's trouble. It's equivalent to a strike. A strike is an action by one part of a business against the other part to gain some advantage. Well, what do you think a husband is doing when he goes on a three-day drunk after a family quarrel? That's a strike, friend, pure and simple. Or consider the woman who walks out of the bedroom in a huff and sleeps on the couch. Isn't she striking against her business partner? The silent treatment that lasts a week, a legal separation, and a divorce threat are all ways a mate strikes against unfair treatment.

I saw a gentleman today who is on the verge of getting a divorce. He protested that his wife repeatedly ignored his wishes. When she did not remember that he wanted his peace and quiet at suppertime and wanted only to listen to problems after the meal, he felt hurt and rejected. The resentment was bottled up because he didn't want to be a dictator. He felt he didn't want her cooperation if he had to demand it of her. She was supposed to do it on her own because she agreed with him. He was bitter that he had to tell her what changes he wanted, such as not overprotecting the youngest boy. She was supposed to know what he wanted and he would not confront her with his wishes more than a few times. If she needed to be pushed, he didn't want her favors.

It was at this point that I too protested with the following argument. "Consider your marriage as a business. You married your wife in the hopes she would be the kind of mate you've always dreamed of. To get her to understand what you want, you must tell her in no uncertain terms and you may have to do it repeatedly."

"But what if she does it only because I tell her to? Who wants it that way?" he insisted.

"You do," I replied. "You work in a factory and have gone on strike. Don't tell me for one moment that you're squeamish about the benefits you get from your company simply because you've gotten benefits against its will. I can't believe you mind very much bringing your grievances to the attention of management. You're out for certain benefits and you fight for them.

"Now think of your marriage as a business. You're working for your company and you want some changes. If you don't feel hurt when the place you work doesn't anticipate all your needs, why should you feel hurt if your wife does the same thing? If you accept a raise that you forced the company to give you, why should it bother you to be firm with your wife? Unless you get some important desires fulfilled on your job or in your marriage, you'll soon be unhappy in both. And when that happens you'll want to strike, just like you've already done.

"This view may sound callous and selfish, but I prefer to think of it as healthy self-interest. And unless you look out for these interests most important to you, whether your mate offers them without being asked makes no difference. You'll become so unhappy with your marriage, you'll turn against it. This will lead to trouble or divorce. In the meanwhile, because you are tolerating mistreatment, your mate will lose respect for you. And when that happens, love dies too."

I continued to debate with my client in the hopes that he would return home, stand up for his needs, and thus preserve the marriage. It has been my experience that men and women who give in repeatedly ultimately become so frustrated and unhappy they regret it. Marriage is an arrangement wherein two self-interests are weighed against each other repeatedly. Seldom sacrifice yourself to the point where you're miserable while your mate is blissful. Most marriages cannot survive one mate happy and the other dejected. The old-fashioned notion that women were supposed to devote themselves selflessly to their husbands is utter nonsense. The happy marriage is the one in which the happiness is shared about equally. Anything less leads to depression and other emotional symptoms: infidelity, alcoholism, child abuse, and that sad, empty feeling that you have made a serious mistake and may not be able to correct it without turning your life upside down.

To avoid this condition, consider two further insights that have come out of marriage counseling and rational-emotive psychotherapy. The first is that you are usually better off deciding important

19

issues with your head than with your heart. This may sound like blasphemy but my experience has proved it correct time after time. To think with your feelings is to think with no reason at all. Emotional thinking is frequently irrational thinking.

The wife who repeatedly drives down to the tavern to pick up her inebriated husband is thinking only with her heart. She does not consider how she is rewarding her husband for his irresponsible behavior. He will call upon her again and again whenever he has had too much to drink, if he knows she will respond.

Were she to think with her head, she would not hesitate to refuse to treat him like a child who needs mama. The hell with that, she would think. If he can't control his drinking, then let him stay at the saloon until he sobers up. Let him suffer the consequences of his irresponsible behavior until he learns to accept responsibility for his actions. To give in to his maneuvering is ultimately more dangerous than it is to try to control it.

The husband who insists that he has the right to chase every skirt he's attracted to (but his wife better not even smile at another man) is thinking with his feelings, not his head. He may insist that he's a fair man, believing in equality, and that he could not tolerate being treated with discrimination. And he thinks he's being reasonable. But just ask him if it's all right for his wife to have affairs (which have been acceptable for him) and he protests like a stuck pig. That's thinking with your emotions, not your head. Who needs it?

The second myth that needs exploding is that a couple, if they love each other enough, will be conflict-free for most of their marriage. All they have to do is arrive at an understanding (guided by their intense love for each other) and everything will be hunky-dory forever thereafter. Wrong!

The vast majority of marriages are arrangements fluctuating between war and peace for the duration of the union. There may be quiet periods for months or years. But count on it, sooner or later there will be wishes and demands by one mate that clash seriously with those of the other. Not only are these periodic wars inevitable in most marriages, I also contend they are healthy. Nothing remains the same for long, not even your blissful honeymoon. Human beings, being what they are, want changes. When that happens, watch out.

Sue was a real sweetheart as long as she ironed Jim's shirts, stayed home with the kids, and didn't complain about the hours he kept. Then one day she decided to improve her education by attending a psychology class at the local junior college. The marriage, that peaceful and ideal relationship which everyone envied, exploded into warfare. He stomped and fumed and cussed her seventeen different ways for daring to ask him to baby-sit and for daring to become more informed than he.

That was the beginning of a long conflict. She was fighting for her rights and for an improvement of the family over the insipid arrangement they had before. Her confrontation was a healthy act that led her to even things up a bit. When she gained some advantage she felt better and the marriage improved. That's what an occasional dispute accomplishes. Such battles between the sexes are necessary—unfortunately.

OTHER COMMON MYTHS BRIEFLY EXAMINED

There has to be more wishful thinking about marriage than possibly any other institution. Some commonly held assumptions are humorous, some plain silly, but all of them wrong or even dangerous.

1. One is that marriage will settle a person down and get those wild ways out of his system. Maybe! Often as not, especially if the groom-to-be is still young, he's likely to have a lot of pizzazz to get out of his system. It amazes me that so many girls in their late teens or early twenties find, after a few months of marriage, that honey isn't coming home any more right after work. He's stopping off with the boys for a few beers at the local bar. Others leave their young brides to join the gang on their motorcycles and ride around until long after dark, sometimes with women. The desire to chase skirts is not out of their systems merely because they're married.

Some people settle down when married, many don't. If you don't see evidence of a serious desire to become domesticated before marriage, wait until you do see it, or give up and seek someone else.

2. Another myth is that marriage will automatically make two persons happier than they have ever been. Wrong! Marriage will bring more frustrations than you dreamed of. It can make you happier than you have ever been too, but to achieve that, you're going to go through lots of tight moments. There will be constant ups and downs between the two of you, and sometimes you won't reach the kind of adjustment you've always expected for literally years after you marry. One woman stayed with her alcoholic husband for twenty years before they ironed out their troubles. In short, after you marry, expect periodic flare-ups. Never be naive enough to think that everything is going to be smooth just because you're very much in love.

3. Another pipe dream is that there is only one person in the world who was made just for you. If you'll recall my definition of love, you'll see how mistaken this idea is. There are literally many people with whom you could fall in love. If someone satisfies your needs and deepest wishes, you'll fall in love again, and again, and again. And each of these loves can be deep and genuine. The next time you hear someone ask, "Can I love two people at the same time?" your answer can be, "Yes, two or two dozen (if you get around enough)."

4. Another myth is that if your mate loves you, he or she will practically always do what you want. You're forgetting that your mate may be saying the same and expecting *you* to give in, if you love him or her as much as you've been insisting.

Billy was angry with Mabel because she wouldn't accept his week-long hunting trips. But she too felt he wasn't very loving if he didn't see her need to go on her annual shopping trip with her girl friends to the big city. Who's right? Neither. The question always is: To whom is the issue most important? If Mabel senses that her husband's trip is more important to him than her shopping is to her, then he ought to get his way. And the same applies to Billy. The greater desire is determined by recognizing how much you want something as compared to how much he or she wants something. That takes time, discussion, and compromise. When you say, "If you really loved me, you'd ———," and your mate

22

answers, "But if you loved me, you wouldn't ———," know immediately you're guiding yourselves by a popular myth about marriage. *+ Trouble*

5. A similar assumption insists that real lovers don't have quarrels. A most attractive and intelligent couple once counseled with me for, of all things, not being able to argue out the problems in their marriage.

They were so polite toward each other that they never had a cross word. They literally *never* spoke loudly when in disagreement. They could juggle a teacup and talk about the most frustrating problems: money, in-laws, friends, and jobs. When Jacob felt quite jealous of Betty's attentions to a handsome guest at a recent party, he was too civil to tell her outright how rejected and threatened he felt. Instead he charged into the issue with:

"Honey, did you enjoy your conversation with Mark Hall last night?"

"Why, yes, I did. Didn't you find him interesting?"

"Really, I didn't talk to him that much. I was just worried that some of our other guests might have felt slightly ignored. More tea?"

"No, thank you, sweetheart."

"Let's see, where were we? Oh, yes, I wanted to warn you that Mark has a way with women. Do be careful, won't you?"

"Oh, Jacob, you're such an alarmist," she said lightly, not even beginning to realize how upset her husband actually was.

Jacob and Betty were brought up never to quarrel with raised voices. The sign of sophistication and maturity was supposedly the art of polite talk under all circumstances. I can certainly applaud nonviolent and civil talk between two persons, but hardly when it gets so polite the real message never gets through. For example, Jacob did not let his wife know that he strongly disliked her flirting. Instead, he suggested that Mark was the aggressor. Jacob also ached to tell Betty he never wanted her to invite Mark again but thought this too crude. He wanted to tell her a great deal more, about other things he never spoke of. But this conversation, like all the others, settled nothing because it addressed itself to nothing.

Even though you are strongly in love with your mate, he or she will give you enough problems during the life of your marriage to

23

fill a book. Love is no guarantee against conflicts in marriage. In every marriage, as in every business, these matters are better confronted head on. If you can be diplomatic while pressing your point, all the better. But be firm at all costs, not angry. A quarrel doesn't have to be an ugly affair, even if voices are raised, any more than a labor dispute between a union and management has to get down to name-calling and fist-throwing.

In my experience the best marriages are those which deal with problems honestly and openly. The complaint is registered in straightforward language. Jacob could have addressed Betty as follows: "Honey, I saw you spending a lot of time with Mark last night. I think you showed bad taste to our other guests and I got very jealous. Would you kindly not do that again?"

Betty might respond with: "But, sweetheart, you're upsetting yourself over nothing. I don't think I cornered Mark as you insist. I was merely amusing Mark as I try to make all my guests comfortable. You don't ever have to feel jealous of me. I resent that."

"You may be right, Betty, but I must ask you nevertheless to recognize my jealous streak and not give me cause to worry."

"I will, but you have to make a concession too."

"What's that?"

"Get counseling."

These lovers are solving their difficulties, not just complaining about them. Such scenes are regrettable, perhaps, but they are necessary. Pressing your point may save the marriage, not destroy it. It is a myth to believe that real lovers never quarrel.

6. It is also a myth to believe that women love men who cater to them practically all the time. Young men are especially guilty of following this piece of nonsense. The high school boy wants to make a big hit with his girl, so he asks her which show she would like to see. Later he asks her where she wants to go for an ice-cream soda. All evening and every time they're out together, he tries to demonstrate his boundless love by politely giving in to each and every wish that enters her pretty head. How can he lose, he reasons?

Easy. Little does he realize that he is handling his dumpling all wrong. Instead of appearing like a gallant knight to his girl, the

24

young fellow (or any adult male as far as that goes) is looking more and more like a chump.

That's right. Believe it or not, women do not respect the man who gives in to their every whim. I once found this difficult to understand. I was always pleased if someone gave me my way most of the time. To me it meant I was liked and wanted as a friend. Therefore, in my practice when I repeatedly came across women who lost respect for men who were very good to them, I asked a lot of questions. Here is what I found.

Women value security more than indulgence. When they make requests of their boyfriends, fiancés, or husbands, they don't mind *some* of their wishes being granted but not all of them. They want men who can say no to them, who are strong enough to stand being rejected, who won't allow the women to wrap them around their little fingers. That scares the ladies because they suddenly realize that they haven't found a man, but a boy.

At first they can't be sure of that. So, to find out what their men are made of they make increasing demands, hoping each time that these fellows will show some backbone and deny them. In their hearts the gals want the men to stand up to them some of the time and prove their independence.

"But," you insist, "if that were the case, why do women protest so loudly when their men don't give them their way? If women really wanted their partners to refuse them, then why aren't they pleased when that's exactly what they do?"

Ah! That's the rub. I've found that women only playact when they stamp their feet, shove out their lower lips, or shed a few tears. They're testing you, buddy, they're testing you. If you can stand up to *that* test, you'll earn her respect. If you give in at that point, she comes on stronger the next time, acting real mad because you've refused her, but all the while secretly (or even unconsciously) wishing you'd take a firm stand.

If you want to win the woman in your life, be gentle, considerate, and tender. But don't overdo it. Get her respect first, *then* you'll earn her love. Respect comes first, love second. And you get her respect by showing her that you don't *need* her even though she's very important to you. That's what she's looking for, proof

25

that you're man enough to live without her. If she can't push you around, then others won't be able to push you around either. If you're mature enough to handle that, she has good reason to feel comfortable in your company. Remember? Women want security before indulgence. So be nice to your lady, but don't be a pushover.

7. A final myth is that any marriage can work if you work at it hard enough. When you consider the possibilities of making a good match out of all the choices you have at your disposal, you have to agree that a happy marriage is a miracle. Yet, many people believe that a good marriage is always possible if the couple works at it hard enough. Then, if they divorce, they feel guilty over not having tried hard enough. The thing they don't understand is that some marriages just aren't made in heaven and no amount of effort and patience is going to make them work.

It comes down to this: There are basically two kinds of marriages. The one is workable because both parties are compatible but may not get along from time to time because of their separate neurotic problems. If they can work out their difficulties by themselves or with the guidance of a counselor, their marriage can return to the harmony it once had.

The second type of marriage is the one that should never have taken place to begin with. The differences between the two persons can be so wide that no amount of understanding will bring them together unless one of them gives up his or her deepest principles.

For example, if you believe that people are decent, that it is important to be honest, and that there is a God in heaven, you are bound to have a devil of a time living with a mate who thinks that all people are crooks, that it is perfectly fine to cheat if you can get away with it, and who has no religion. Is it conceivable that these persons from two different worlds can find happiness under the same roof? I don't see how.

Every time they discuss anything important to either of them they're bound to clash. Every time a quarrel arises between their children, their opposing views of morality are bound to turn each other into enemies pronto. Each values his or her own beliefs. They're not likely to give them up easily and certainly not for the opposing views of the mate. It's a wonder these people get together at all. Sometimes a couple is so eager to marry and so blinded by

26

love that these dangerous discrepancies aren't noticed. It's only later that the trouble shows up.

Other couples don't realize that they are strongly incompatible until a number of years after they are married. When their views and philosophies have matured, they begin to realize that they are heading in different directions.

What to do about such marriages? They can be tolerated and made the most of because divorce is forbidden for religious or financial reasons. Counseling does the mates little good because they made a mistake to marry at all. A divorce is actually one of the more civil solutions open to them.

Let's face it, hard work and good intentions can achieve wonders, but every so often even they are powerless to help a marriage that is a mistake. It's a myth to believe that all troubled marriages can be helped.

Chapter 2

The Real Reasons
for Marrying

You don't marry for love. You marry because you expect certain important behavior from your mate, and when you get it, you fall in love. It therefore becomes important to look into the goals people seek in marriage. Some of these goals are healthy, some neurotic. Either way, however, love is the prize. That's right. Even people marrying for sick reasons can love their mates for the sick things they do for them just as healthy people love their mates for the kind things their mates do for them.

Let's look first at the neurotic reasons for marrying.

NEUROTIC REASONS FOR MARRYING

To Spite Your Parents

This particular piece of neurotic behavior comes mostly from teen-agers who are told by their well-meaning parents that they can't marry. This is like waving a red flag in front of a bull. Tell them they should brush their teeth and the young rebels invite cavities. Order them to study hard so they can have a fine education and they refuse to open their books. Refuse to let them date for fear they'll come home diseased or pregnant and they sneak out the bedroom window. And refuse to give them permission to marry and they get themselves into such a fix you have no choice but to go along. That, or they elope.

We call this the power struggle. Parents insist they're more powerful than their children, while the children insist they're more

28

powerful than the parents. Who's right? Hold onto your pride—
the children are right. If your advice and usual authority won't
control your children, there's no way this side of sanity you're
going to get them to behave sensibly. They'll have to get hurt in
the manner you predicted they would be hurt. I know that it may
be too late to save them from one harm but after they spitefully
defy you they may wake up enough to take your advice at a later
date. Little consolation, I agree, but what choice do you have?

Marrying against their parents' will is one of those classical
power plays young people sometimes get involved in. They want
to marry, not because they're so absolutely taken by their future
mates, but to spite their parents, to show them up, or to put them
down. What better way to humiliate and anger their parents than
to see them helplessly pleading for the young couple to delay? And
what of the poor bride or groom who is not aware of this conscious
or unconscious strategy being played upon him or her by the lover?
The innocent victim thinks the marriage is for love when the truth
is that spite is the real motive behind that wedding.

Years later the one who married out of spite may increasingly
feel it was a mistake but be too embarrassed to admit it. So the
spiteful mate goes on being miserable. Oh, love, your disguises are
unlimited!

To Overcome an Inferiority Complex

She is a shy little thing, not very popular even though she's
pretty. She has earned good grades in her four years in high school.
Academically she feels secure but socially she's inferior. Not until
she met Dick, the handsome and popular class president, did she
enter the charmed circle. It never fooled her, however, why she was
more accepted. Her steady boyfriend pulled her into the limelight
and she knew it. At his side she felt secure. On her own she walked
down the halls alone.

Had she used his company as a ladder to growth, she could have
profited greatly in changing her negative self-image. However, she
still saw herself as nothing unless in his company and receiving his
approval. A warm look, a kind word from him made this Cinder-
ella feel like a princess. When he responded a year after graduation

with a proposal for marriage, she could not resist.

Of course she was in love. Millions of young people have waltzed down the aisle for precisely this neurotic reason: marriage to build up the ego. Why is this neurotic? Because no one else can make you feel worthwhile. The feeling of inferiority comes from thinking you are bad because some of your behavior is bad. That's called self-blame. It creates guilt, depression, and inferiority. It makes no difference where you are, who you're with, or how well you behave, if you're a self-blamer and aren't outstanding in those actions you value highly, you'll feel inferior. Being married to Mr. or Ms. Wonderful is not going to change your condition except for the short while you are receiving approval. Just let your lover get a bit angry at you and all your inferiority comes back.

Dick thinks his wife loves him. Technically she loves the feeling of being a somebody in his company. If he withdraws that support, she'll be upset and eventually lose that feeling of love. The unspoken contract she accepted with the wedding vows is that he must continue to make her feel superior. That's why she hired him —to combat her feeling of being a nothing.

A sad development can sometimes occur in a marriage based on this contract. In the early stages, our young, shy flower will adore her young god because he's untarnished, can do nothing wrong, and she always feels better in his company. But Dick is not a god. He is a fine young man, with the emphasis on young. He's not perfect. He can't make her happy all the time. There are times when he goofs off, when he's awkward and inexperienced as a husband. His wife, upon seeing these developments, begins to fear the worst and that can end the honeymoon.

If you want to overcome feelings of inferiority, then take the responsibility for your problem and work at correcting it. Don't rely on others to do your job for you. If you want to marry someone who can teach and support you in your growth, well and good. But never dump that problem totally on your mate. Ultimately, even with help, the chore falls to you. To expect otherwise is neurotic and will lead to a marriage of disappointment and divorce quicker than you can say "I do."

To Be a Therapist for Your Mate

Ever hear of a therapeutic marriage? Probably not, but I'll bet your tranquilizers you've seen enough of them. It's a marriage based on the unspoken contract that one partner will play the part of the parent, the other the child.

If you have a need to feel important, and you have a heart as big as a mountain, you're a first-class candidate for a therapeutic marriage. Watch out. In this case love is defined as the opportunity to relate to someone who is sick, weak, or childish. Such a person will bring out your nursing and mothering instincts like nothing you've ever seen. Another name for this type of marriage is the Florence Nightingale marriage. Bear in mind, a man can fall into this trap too; he can nurse his wife as easily as a woman can nurse a man.

In a therapeutic marriage you want your mate to be unstable, insecure, unable to make decisions, and the more immature he or she is the better. Were it any other way, you wouldn't be attracted to that person. He or she must be inadequate to qualify. Can you imagine such a mess? Yet such is often the case, for your feeling of being superior comes most easily in the company of someone who is inferior.

This is why some women marry men who drink. The wife may complain from time to time about her husband's irresponsibility, his need to be helped into bed, and even bailed out of jail. Later she can give him hell and establish her superiority again. As long as this behavior doesn't get out of hand, the marriage can continue on its merry way with mother scolding her adolescent, all the while loving the importance she gains from this, and he feels secure that someone cares for him and still wants to look after his interests.

The amount of abuse this type of marriage can absorb is really amazing. Sylvia tolerated Roger's gambling, forcing her thereby to get a job to pull the family out of debt. When he smashed up the family car and lost his license it meant she could use the second car to drive him to work. So far so good. Sylvia felt powerful in these acts of sacrifice. She rose to each occasion like a Trojan and knew it. What's more, her friends and family continually compli-

31

mented her on how well she handled each crisis. Sylvia was in her glory. Then Roger stepped out on her. This was something she hadn't counted on. It was her Achilles' heel and she didn't know how to handle it. No longer did she want to tolerate his irresponsibilities when they reached this stage. Such behavior made her look bad, not good, and it immediately reduced her love for Roger. No longer would she be able to be his therapist or mother. With this behavior he entered forbidden territory.

Not all therapeutic marriages need to end in disaster. If the stronger mate really wants the weaker mate to grow up, he or she will not always rescue the drinker, gambler, or ne'er-do-well. Instead (to use the example of Sylvia and Roger again), she could have helped him by refusing to bail him out of jail. Let him sit until he realizes it's going to be up to him to stay out of trouble. When he lost his job she would have been wiser to cook up another batch of goulash, not go out and get a job. In this way the boy might have grown into manhood. But Sylvia would have had to adjust to this growth on his part. If she wants him to change, she'll have to change too.

My advice to these charitable Florence Nightingales is to look reality squarely in the face. When your fiancé shows certain objectionable symptoms before marriage, it's safe to conclude you're likely to get the same behavior after marriage. Stop thinking love conquers all. It doesn't.

If your girl friend is a wild spender now, be prepared for big bills later. If your boyfriend is tardy now or he doesn't notify you if there is a change in plans, be prepared for similar behavior later.

I'm not suggesting that people can't change, only that you'll have a problem that only a lot of hard work will overcome. Don't fool yourself, for example, by believing that he won't show you disrespect if you notice that he treats his parents with disrespect. He may be as sweet as honey while he's dating you, but once the ring is on your finger he may also slip one through your nose. Rude behavior is part of his personality and you and all your good intentions may just not be enough to change habits which require professional help.

Fear of Spinsterhood or Bachelorhood

Nothing seems to propel some young folks into marriage more quickly than the fear they will never marry at all if they don't take advantage of the first opportunity. That seems to be one of the reasons seniors in high school or recent graduates jump at the chance. They view being single as a failure to equal their friends' achievement. When those wedding bells start breaking up that old gang, those who are left sometimes get chicken and run to the altar so as not to be humiliated.

Parents often push their children into an early marriage either to get them off their hands or to overcome their fears the kids won't ever get married. They fail to realize that not being married is nothing to fear or be ashamed of. The day will come soon enough to many of those who married early when they will realize they were hasty.

Psychologically, the reason young people follow the leader in matrimony is that they judge themselves by their achievements. They reason, incorrectly, that a failure to catch a mate means that they are total failures. They judge themselves by their behavior, a serious mistake. You are never the same as your actions. If you fail a task, you fail a task. That's all, nothing more. You are never a failure as a person because you fail at a popularity contest or because you might be rejected by your friends.

That's right. Rejection does *not* hurt unless you let it. In fact, no one can disturb you unless you let it happen. People can hurt you physically to be sure. They can shoot and stab you, run over you, hit you, or starve you. They can break your bones, make you bleed, and hurt your insides. But they can't hurt your feelings by making you angry, depressed, nervous, or humiliated. Only you can do that to yourself.

When you think you're worthless because you too can't brag about a flashy engagement ring, you're putting yourself through a neurotic wringer. A man may believe he's loved for all kinds of reasons, but will probably not understand that he is being used to overcome the woman's fear of being different. They may eventually make it a good marriage but not until she has grown beyond this neurotic reason for marrying.

Fear of Independence

One of the most neurotic reasons for marrying early is to avoid growth. Becoming an adult is always somewhat painful, and people use endless schemes to avoid it. Some get sick easily and bow out of competition rather than face its risks. Some beg off trying for fear they would fail. There are all sorts of strategies for not facing the hazards of growing up. Marrying early is one of them.

This applies particularly to girls. What better way to avoid finding out what a girl can do than to set up house at seventeen? She can now stop going to school, perhaps not go to work, become pregnant, and raise a family. I know it's not easy to raise a family and I don't want the women to think I'm putting them down. But the adolescent girl who opts for this course doesn't know that. She thinks everything is going to be just fine, that she's got it made. Little does she realize that her young husband, unskilled and miles from his career goals, will probably be too immature to assume his husbandly and fatherly duties. She'll find him hanging around the corner with the boys. He'll have a lot of playing around to do, will want to booze it up with the gang, and not with his young bride present. She'll be at home in the small apartment with perhaps her new baby to keep her company. Is it small wonder the divorce rate is higher with the younger set?

Those young women who leap from the dependent relationship with parents to the dependent relationship with a husband may never experience earning their own money, getting their own home, or their own car. They won't travel or meet the many interesting people their single friends will meet. And most of all, they won't have as much fun.

When you come right down to it, these young women marry out of fear, out of a distrust of facing life alone for a time. They marry men whom they see as strong and on whom they can lean. Usually there's nothing so wrong with that. In their cases, however, they do so, not to grow but to avoid growth. These are the same girls

34

who, when they're in their thirties, break loose and want to grab from life all they missed as kids. They missed dating a variety of fellows, going to parties, traveling, and meeting interesting people at work. Later they often want to finish their education.

For young people who want to marry before you've tasted life I have this advice: Run like hell. You'll thank me for it someday. When you're older, possibly in your mid-twenties, you will be more mature and ready for that great event which can make you happy and fulfilled: a healthy marriage.

The big mistake you'll make if you marry because you *want* to continue your childlike dependency on someone stronger is this: you can't get strong, leaning on others. The more you depend upon yourself the more secure you'll feel. Learn to make decisions on your own, make your mistakes, profit by your errors, and try again. Keep that up over a period of years and eventually you'll feel pretty secure in your decisions. If you sit back and let your spouse run your life, he or she will get more self-confidence while you become less and less confident.

On the Rebound

This is a particularly sad reason for marrying because it is committed for two neurotic reasons, not just one. Let's say you lost out in a love affair. You could find yourself married to someone else surprisingly soon (1) to spite the person who refused you and (2) to prove to yourself that you are still desirable and lovable to someone.

The rebound marriages I have encountered have not usually fared well. They are consummated under a cloud of doubt over one's desirability and the pain of rejection. When such marriages do work, I feel it is more good luck than good planning which is responsible.

Especially sad is the dishonesty being put upon the innocent victim. He or she has been led to believe that the prior affair is a dead issue and that this new love thrives on merits all its own. Such is not the case however if, while walking down the aisle, the bride is having thoughts of revenge and spite against her former boyfriend. That's unfair because it uses the groom for her petty ends, something that might easily appall him if he but knew what was really happening.

If you find yourself falling in love soon after you have fallen out of love, be skeptical of that feeling. The chances of it being neurotically and spitefully motivated are pretty high. Give yourself time to get over the former affair. When you can talk about it calmly without getting uptight or tearful, when you actually don't think of your former love very often and are able to enjoy activities and people, and especially when you can see your old flame and treat the encounter as you would the meeting of a good friend and little more, then you're ready for another serious relationship—marriage included.

Fear of Hurting the Other Person

Not until I became a psychotherapist did I learn that a number of people marry despite strong feelings of wanting to break off the affair. They go through with it because of the intense guilt they would feel over the hurt they would have caused the other person.

"I never should have married Oscar," Mabel told me during one of our sessions. "I tried to get out of it several times but couldn't."

"Why not?" I asked.

"Oscar acted so hurt he actually got sick. Sometimes he'd cry. And when I really made up my mind to end our affair once, he told me he couldn't live without me and he'd kill himself if I didn't marry him. What could I do?"

"You could have been honest, broken off the affair, and placed the responsibility for his future behavior in his lap where it belonged."

"But how was I supposed to live with the guilt of driving him to his death?" she asked with great feeling.

"By realizing that you could not do that. You couldn't have driven him to suicide even if you had wanted to. In fact, to carry it a point further, you weren't even responsible for his getting upset over your rejection. That was all his doing, not yours. He upset himself, not by your plans, but by what he told himself about your plans. In other words, people always upset themselves. You are

36

never correct and justified to blame yourself for their neurotic reactions to your behavior."

"I'll have to think that over. It sounds right and just like what I'd like to hear. So, what should I have told him years ago and what should I tell him now when he tries to make me feel guilty?"

"Tell him you're sorry that he is upsetting himself over your behavior but that you have no intention of changing your mind just because he's upset. If he wants to get over his disturbance, it'll be up to him to change his neurotic thinking to healthy thinking. And if he can't do that by himself, tell him to get instruction from a psychotherapist on how to do it. If he won't do that, tell him to read a good book on the subject."

This advice is good for you too. If you're easily manipulated by people trying to control you through guilt, learn about the new principles of psychology. You'd be amazed at how wrong and just plain foolish you've been for years for allowing others to run your life with emotional blackmail. Don't do it.

Because You Were in Love or Had Sex

Folk wisdom sometimes has a way of turning out to be folk nonsense. I remember once counseling a sweet young thing who was twice divorced but getting ready to marry again. In each case she not only married out of love, but oddly enough, *because* of love. She had the strange idea that once she felt the strings of her heart vibrate she had to marry the fellow. Love simply led to marriage, she thought. It was as simple as that.

It mattered not to her that she didn't know her husbands very well, that some obvious incompatibilities were bound to give her trouble, and that she could just as easily have fallen in love with a few others if she had given herself the chance. She automatically listened to her heart and felt compelled by advice from her childhood, that love and marriage go together like a horse and carriage. And now she was ready to do it for the third time.

Another variation of this theme, at least with older women, is that a girl should marry a man if she has intercourse with him. To do any less would suggest promiscuity. That's the way many females believed a few decades ago and maybe some even do today.

It makes little sense, however, and I'm glad to see this piece of folk "wisdom" fade away.

To Escape an Unhappy Home

When a teen-ager has been yelled at for years, when Mother has been a witch or Dad a drunk, it's easy to see why the child would long to pack up and get out. Boys join the service, hitchhike to Alaska, or hop aboard a tramp steamer headed for South Africa. The moment they are of age they seek to escape the sad and sometimes crazy homelife to which they've been subjected. Sometimes they get a job locally and immediately look for someone to love them as they always wanted to be loved at home.

Girls are more prone to use marriage as an escape from a shoddy homelife. Until recently they couldn't join the services as readily, it's dangerous for them to hitchhike, and women aren't hired on most tramp steamers. So, all that's left to a girl is to attach herself to someone who loves her and promises her a better life. Sometimes she loves him too but that isn't necessary. All she really wants is to be rescued from the horrors of living with impossible parents.

Why not? What does she have to lose? Maybe plenty. If she's lucky and marries well, her troubles could be over. More likely, however, she'll go from the frying pan into the fire. Persons who desperately want to escape a bad scene can't be choosers. They want to be rescued at any price, and sometimes they must pay almost any price for it. They convince themselves that they'll fall in love in time, that his or her bad faults will change if they show enough love. They think matters can only go up since they're at the bottom now.

The truth is that tolerating a bad home until you can support yourself makes the most sense. You are probably too hurt and sensitive, too angry and bitter, too confused and young to make a good mate for anyone. When you have lived with neurotic parents for years, get away to some peace and quiet. Give yourself a chance to recover from those troubled years, and *then* consider marriage if you're so inclined.

HEALTHY REASONS FOR MARRYING

Your chances of having a good marriage depend on how much of your decision to marry was determined by some of the neurotic reasons listed above, and on how much was determined by one or more of the rational and mature reasons listed below.

Companionship

A mate is, above and beyond everything else, someone whose company you enjoy immensely. The person you marry had better be like a great friend to you, a pal, like one of the boys, or one of the girls, if you want a happy marriage. When you aren't having sex, when you don't need a wage earner or a cook, the single most important quality you will seek in your lover is companionship.

The couple who plays tennis together stays together. I don't know if this statement is really true, but it wouldn't surprise me if it turned out to be so. Of course I could have said it differently. The couple who gardens together, swims together, hikes, skis, or plays bridge together, stays together.

It's the couple who has little in common with each other, who shares few mutual interests, that is in trouble in the same way that you'd be unhappy in a law firm if you wanted to paint. Marriage is a business, and the more the employees of that business have pursuits in common, the better they will get along.

I find companionship to be such an enormously important goal in marriage that I must emphasize it for those romantics who constantly confuse love with companionship.

The romantic (in the worst sense of the word) loves his girl friend for reasons he can only vaguely describe. She may be feeding into a number of neurotic needs and for this he adores her. He wants her with him always and cannot conceive of life without her. However, will she make good company for him? That's a totally different story, one he hasn't given much thought to.

To find out if you enjoy your mate's company, notice how you feel in his or her absence. Do you miss her cooking, his handiwork, sex, or the favors he or she usually agrees to? If so, you don't necessarily miss your mate's company because you could hire most of those things done.

If you go to dinner together and you manage to keep the conversation moving for most of the dinner, I'd say you enjoy each other's company.

When you and your spouse take a long drive together, are there silences that stretch practically from the moment the car leaves the driveway to the moment it arrives at the destination? If so, you may not enjoy each other as friends.

In short, if you can't keep each other's company without going to bed, working on a project, or having people visit you, then companionship is not one of the strong points in your marriage. That feeling of *liking* to be with your best pal is a good assurance that you have made a good marital choice. Never mind how good-looking your mate is, or how wealthy, or how considerate, or anything else. If all those fine qualities don't add up to your wanting that person's company, forget it.

A Safe and Convenient Sex Life

Let's face it, men and women marry because they can satisfy their sexual needs better that way than any other.

"But," you ask, "since when is it necessary to be married to have a sex life?"

It isn't necessary to be married to have a sex life, that's not what I said. But it is almost always better to be married if you want that sex to be reasonably safe and convenient. While the married man or woman merely snuggles up close to the partner to begin sexual overtures, the single person must go through a series of rituals before he gets his love into bed that would make the coronation of a king look puny by comparison.

Sex in marriage is not merely more free of disease, but it involves less difficulty in the case of unwanted pregnancy. People caught in this issue while unmarried face some of the most ugly decisions they will ever confront: marry the girl? divorce the husband? get an abortion? break up both families? go through with the pregnancy and raise the child as her own? place the child for adoption?

tell the husband it isn't his? tell him it is his? And so on. The married couple, by comparison, merely decides to have or not to have a baby and proceeds from there. That's convenience.

Marriage Is Still the Best Institution for Raising Children

There have been many experiments for bringing up children, some of which have excluded the natural parents. In China the state is taking over more and more of the rearing of its children. So is the kibbutz in Israel. Some success can be claimed for diminishing the role of the parents, but all in all there seems to be no clear advantage in giving children over to others as compared to the parents' rearing them.

Most couples want children and, more importantly, they want to be the ones who raise these children. And if the parents do a good job of parenting, the joy of raising children can be as great as the joy of having been raised by loving and sensible parents. Few memories are as precious or as enduring as those of our families when we were growing up. No school or academy and no room full of other children each caring for the other can provide the bliss that comes from a kiss, an embrace, and a loving word from a parent or guardian.

The fact that more and more couples are opting not to have families these days simply strengthens my point. It means that more adults who like children are having them and those who don't like them are not having them. This tends to eliminate that percentage of adults in the past who were parents many times over but regarded the role as a burden.

To Achieve a Unique Life-Style

Our society favors the married person. You *and* your spouse are more likely to be invited for dinner than you alone. Therefore if you want to be part of the social life of your community, it's more easily done as a couple.

But so are many other pursuits more readily obtained in a marriage, especially for women. Judy knew she always wanted to be a part of a small-town college society. She was bright, educated,

41

and enjoyed being with stimulating people. But she did not have the money or the drive to get an advanced degree and then get herself hired on the faculty of a college with ivy-covered walls. She loved the atmosphere where people wore tweeds, went to the football games on Saturdays followed by cocktails at a friend's home, and where life was peaceful and dignified.

So what was Judy to do? Marriage was the obvious answer. And marry she did, but not to just anyone. She married the dean of a college. In one stroke she achieved a style of living that gave her everything she ever wanted.

Shrewd? You bet it was. She knew what she wanted and wouldn't settle for less. Being charming and attractive made this possible, of course. But it was her determination to get a specific life-style, and no nonsense about it, that really got her what she wanted. She had met a construction engineer who soon proposed marriage to her. He had money, an airplane, and a fine home. The only thing he didn't have was a Ph.D. and a position on a college faculty. She liked the fellow well enough, thought he was quite handsome and intelligent, but he didn't talk about the cultural and academic things she was interested in. When they socialized, it was with people who drank their liquor straight and talked about business. She missed the polite affairs where the guests sipped wine or tea and chatted lightly about a book review or an art exhibit. This made all the difference. Judy might fall in love with any number of people who appealed to her but she wasn't going into business with anyone seriously unless he and she could live the way she had always dreamed. Bravo, Judy!

THERE OUGHT TO BE A LAW

It should be obvious by now that I am strongly opposed to young people marrying. The vast majority of the time they marry for neurotic reasons; they are still developing their characters and may be very different people a few years after marriage than they were before. They are using years which are better spent on self-enjoyment and freedom to shoulder the most crushing kinds of responsibilities—all in the name of love. It's enough to make you cry.

42

There are two regrets people seem to report to me more than any others. Can you guess what they are? Think about it a moment, because the answer may surprise you.

The one regret is: not getting more education. Many people soon learn that their more schooled peers have more secure lives by and large, enjoy more interesting work, and eventually wield more power. Those who scoffed at learning in their youth have a lifetime to spend in regret.

The second regret, even more common than the first, is marrying too young. I have had more than a few emergency calls from depressed clients who, because they were poor, had too many children too early, and were married to immature, selfish, or violent spouses, wanted to die. They also learned that loving someone is one thing: marrying someone is another.

They refused to listen to all the facts that urge them to wait. Love is never more blind than in the young. They know so little but think they know so much. They ignore the fact that the divorce rate rises as the age of marriage goes down. And it is for this reason that I would pass a law, had I the power, to make marriage illegal until about twenty-five. Sounds preposterous? Then why do we place an age limit on driving, drinking, voting, military service, and a number of other pursuits? Because we recognize the great danger involved in letting a ten-year-old order a Scotch and soda, or giving an eighth-grader a 400-horsepower car to race down the highway. Most tasks have a minimum age below which they cannot be performed sensibly or safely.

What about the teen-age girl who gets herself pregnant? That's the rub of course and explains why such laws are not likely to work. But if I thought they would stand half a chance, I'd work for them. To be more realistic, this problem is not going to be corrected with laws as much as by education. When the day comes that people look at love and marriage more realistically, some of the mistakes so prevalent in the past may largely become a thing of the past. That's one of the reasons for writing this book. If it should have the effect of getting people to delay the age of marriage by even one year, I'd feel my effort was worthwhile.

People who marry for the irrational reasons listed in the first part of this chapter are actually emotionally disturbed and require

43

a diagnosis like any other psychological condition. I offer the term _Love neurosis_ to refer to people who are about to do something self-defeating and irrational; who are so blinded by "love" that you fear for their futures.

In summary, it would be infinitely healthier for our society if it were much more difficult to get married and somewhat easier to get divorced.

Chapter 3

Why Marriages Go Sour

For the past year and a half I have kept tally of every couple who has come to me for marital counseling. During the first session I made it a point always to ask one or both partners what was the major cause of distress in the marriage.

Before these data were refined I was given thirty-five reasons for marriage unhappiness. Because some were only a shade different from others, I grouped some together and came out with the following table:

Major Frustrations in Marriage	
Anger and domination	58
Rejection	37
Passivity and dependency	30
Sex	26
Companionship	25
Family	24
Neurotic behavior	15
Total	215

ANGER AND DOMINATION

There are some surprises in this table and there are also confirmations of previous views I've proposed. For example, in my book *Overcoming Frustration and Anger* I pointed out that anger in all its forms is the most frequent disturbed emotion throughout the population. In this table we see married people complaining more often about the incessant anger and unreasonableness of the mate than of any other single factor.

Clients reported that their husbands were usually domineering and angry. Forty-one subjects made that complaint. By itself, it could be the single most frequent frustration in marriages today. Why? For two reasons I believe. First, the man thinks he's king because he's a man. That's what he's been taught for centuries. The second reason we are seeing so many complaints about the husband's hostile behavior is that the women are no longer tolerating it. They have a newfound sense of equality and indignation over being treated unfairly. So they are standing up for their rights and it's driving the men up the wall. If they would not rock the boat and accept things as they were, I'm sure I would have witnessed far fewer reports about angry husbands for the simple reason that they would not have been frustrated over wives seeking equality. But when a woman asks her husband to help with the evening meal after they have both returned home from their jobs, what's a good red-blooded American boy supposed to do? Quietly and peacefully assist her? Not on your life. That's un-American because it isn't man's work. So he yells and storms, but only because she had the audacity to ask. Years ago she would have worked all day at the office, gone home and cooked a meal, washed the dishes, and before retiring put a load of clothes into the washer.

I hope that the ladies don't back down to their angry mates. We men are decent people too, and given time to get used to the new standards, we can learn to live with you and continue to love you even if you don't jump at every command.

A letter from one of my past clients can illustrate what sometimes happens when a doormat of a wife digs her heels into the rug and refuses to be further abused.

Dear Dr. Hauck:

Remember me? I was the slow one in group therapy trying to overcome my husband's domineering ways. I'm doing fine even though he's still the yelling and bossy person. But I take it all as a bunch of noise now. Your recommendations are finally starting to sink in.

He yells but it doesn't last long and I'm not afraid of him anymore and my nerves are more calm. I've learned so much. My only regret is that I didn't get counseling years ago.

After each of my therapy sessions I'd come home and make notes on your remarks. I reread those on occasion and it helps. I'm still a little depressed at times but I handle it by training my thoughts and reading your book [Overcoming Depression]. *I read a lot now, which I thoroughly enjoy, because, when I was depressed I didn't even read the daily paper for a year or so. I just couldn't concentrate.*

Yours truly,

Ms. B.

Those of you (males too) who want to get your angry and dominating mates off your backs must expect minor revolutions when you begin to make your play. They will not take your assertiveness lying down. First they'll start off easy with yelling or accusations, then progress to threats. If this doesn't get you to knuckle under, they may threaten to leave you, divorce you, or have an affair. The final stage gets really sticky with potential physical violence against you or threats of suicide. No matter! If you really want your equality, you're going to have to put up with a lot of pressure until your mate gives in. In the meantime, expect one strategy after the other to be thrown at you in the hopes that you'll cave in. Don't do it. You'll seldom have your mate's respect if you allow yourself to become a doormat. And if you don't have respect, you won't get love either. Your marriage is at stake, so risk it by being firm on your own behalf and you may save it. Give in like a scared rabbit and you can't guarantee your marriage at all, you'll become so unhappy that you eventually won't care whether you're married or not. Then *you* may seek a divorce because you allowed your mate to make you so miserable.

The whole task of standing up for your rights is made easier if you remind yourself that you got into the marriage for certain advantages and that, like any business arrangement, you have a perfect right to complain about broken promises. You'd never feel guilty about wanting a raise, a vacation, good working conditions, and so on, on your job, would you? Then why tolerate abuse in your marriage? Marriage is a business and if you don't run it like one, you'll spend your life making others happy but not making yourself happy. That leads to a bankrupt business (divorce).

REJECTION

The next most frequent frustration in marriage (37) deals with love, jealousy, old flames, and feelings of rejection. It is also under this heading that we deal with the desire to be unfaithful. Four of my subjects realized they married too young and had an intense desire to have other romances.

A frequent result of marrying too young is shown in the fifteen people who were out of love because they found themselves almost completely incompatible with their mates, both philosophically and emotionally. These are the marriages that should never have taken place at all, but the couples were too blinded by who knows what to realize it.

Three of the clients in the Rejection category appear to have married on the rebound since they admitted to having strong feelings of love for their old lovers.

Three other women felt rejected so long by their husbands they gave up ever having a loving relationship again with them. They opted for divorce.

Two subjects claim they never loved their mates and married only for financial security. Unfortunately both their mates had little ambition and this caused respect for them to be lost.

One client had no other complaint in his marriage than that it was boring and lacked fun. He had not counted on the many demands marriage made on his time, or the need to work and even forfeit vacations for extra pay to handle the baby's doctor bills. This insight and many like it left him grossly disillusioned. Playing house is hard, adult work, not kid stuff.

Trying to make your mate feel loved can be a tricky affair at times. Just when you think you've been the sweetheart you were expected to be, you get a blast that singes your ears. Peter reported such a situation. He would cook for Ethel when she wasn't well, regularly took out the garbage, and helped in every way with the children. Still she was unhappy and complained to me of feeling unloved. I confess I was as surprised at this as Peter must have been.

"I came from a family," she said, fighting back the tears, "where I was always criticized. I could do nothing right for my parents. If anything went wrong, they accused me even before they heard my side. Never, but never did they take my side. Peter does the same. He almost always sides with my folks when we have a disagreement and I hate him for it. All the kind things he does for me are completely canceled when he won't defend me. I can't help myself and I know I'm wrong but I honestly can't help it."

Ethel defined love in a very specific way: stick up for me if you care for me. She didn't define it as other women might have: buy me flowers, help with the dishes, don't be jealous, etc. Each person determines for himself or herself what is most important from another and unless you meet *most* of those expectations *most* of the time your marriage is almost bound to be unhappy. So listen and observe your mates *carefully*. They are giving out cues all the time of what is important to them.

Sometimes no matter what you do, your mate will not give you the love you desire. This is especially true if your wife or husband didn't love you when you were first married and you believed your love was enough for both of you. This can work out nicely on rare occasions but it's risky. As one client put it in a moment of insight: "She told me she didn't love me but I didn't believe her. I thought I'd win her somehow but nothing ever clicked."

Small wonder. What he didn't realize was that she had a problem loving any men. Not that she was a lesbian. She just didn't like men for a host of unconscious reasons going back years into her past, reasons which she never understood or explored. Their marriage was almost a hopeless case from the start.

Jealousy was mentioned by five of my subjects as the specific reason for wanting a divorce. Actually it often played an important role in many other marriages, but those couples gave different frustrations as the primary source of discontent and may have mentioned jealousy as a close second. In the above I have listed only the major frustrations identified by my clients as the single most annoying problem in their marriages.

The jealous person is the one who becomes depressed, feels inferior, and gets upset over the very thought that the spouse may be disloyal. Jealousy does not occur merely because you suspect your lover is running around. That may actually be the case. Perhaps you've seen clear evidence of it. Or you know from your mate's past behavior that such an act is not out of the question. In other words your experience and observations of your spouse can accurately at times spot an illicit affair going on. If she occasionally dashes out to the grocery store late at night on what seems to be a weak reason, you could conclude your wife is meeting someone. Your suspicions would grow and have a right to grow, until you could definitely prove or disprove your charge.

But that's not jealousy. Suspicion and jealousy are not the same. When you're jealous, you aren't simply saying that your mate is unfaithful (which may or may not be true) but also that *you* are worthless if he or she prefers another. Rubbish! Not being loved by your mate never reduces you as a human. It is hoped that you are as important to yourself before a rejection as you are after a rejection. No one and nothing can reduce your self-importance but you. The trouble with the jealous person is not that he or she distrusts the mate. Oh, no! It is that he or she distrusts himself or herself. And every jealous person knows this the moment it is explained.

If you think every Tom, Dick, and Harry is capable of beating your time, then you obviously haven't got a lot of confidence in yourself, have you? If you really felt secure that you were desirable, capable, and strong, it would never occur to you to shake in the knees at the thought of losing your love, as unpleasant as that would be.

In short, the jealous person is always admitting an inferiority complex. The meaning of a statement like, "You love someone else, I'm certain of it, and I could kill that person and you too," is this: *"because I am nothing without you."*

Did you ever hear the song "You're Nobody Until Somebody Loves You"? That happens to be the theme song of all the jealous people in the world. It's a nice melody but those lyrics have got to go!

The next time your mate wants to give you the third degree after you've come home three and a half minutes late, don't explain why

50

you're late. Don't get angry. Instead, apologize politely and turn and look your spouse straight in the eyes and say something like: "Dear, you're making yourself jealous again. I thought you were going to do something about getting over those feelings. You must be very upset being always threatened by every little thing I do. Do see someone about this, will you, honey?"

Don't laugh. What better answer for someone who is trying to control every second of your life, every smile, every casual glance? He or she needs help, not an explanation from you. Help your mate change his or her neurosis if you can. Don't take it upon yourself to stand on your head just so your loved one will feel secure for a short while. This will cause you trouble, fights, and long periods of rejection. If you give into it, however, the problem will crop up again the next time the phone rings and no one answers. Your stand should always be: "When *you,* dear mate, don't care for yourself and won't take care of *your* jealousy, then you're in trouble; *not when I don't care.*"

PASSIVITY AND DEPENDENCY

The third set of frustrations were made more often by the wives. Women usually cannot stand weak and dependent men, let alone weak and dependent husbands.

It seems that the women are having a bad time of it, being dissatisfied with bossy, domineering, and stubborn husbands on the one hand, and weak, childlike, and dependent husbands on the other. To be fair, it's got to be hard on the men also. While they try to find the proper balance between being firm and kind, they can easily incur the rejection of their wives if they overstep the bounds on either side.

A caution for couples with this problem: when this problem exists, it's because both of you are permitting it to exist. Some women love to baby and spoil their husbands because it gives them a feeling of importance and power. The trouble with this pattern is that it gets out of hand after a while. The wife doesn't mind babying her husband somewhat, but he, enjoying being her son, wants more spoiling. That's the way it goes until she gets all the responsibility dumped into her lap. At that point it isn't fun anymore and she resents having another child in addition to her young ones. She finds she must consider his wishes in almost all matters. She denies herself to make him happy while he soaks up her efforts as though he were royally entitled to her services.

One such husband simply shut off his senses to his wife's messages, even when she spoke to him in the most direct manner imaginable. She wanted him to take out the garbage, but he procrastinated so long she often did it herself when the pail overflowed. At other times she would be moved by a spurt of hope and literally placed the bag of refuse at his feet at the dinner table. He'd laugh and step over it on his way to work. Years later, after hundreds of such disappointments, she left him. And wouldn't you know it, he was flabbergasted.

Of the thirty subjects who came to me because their mates were undependable, twelve had the specific complaint that they had to give in to their mates all the time, grant their whims to keep them happy, and deny themselves repeatedly. They found that the only way to keep their mates happy was to cater to them. The moment they resisted they had hell to pay. The females would tear the house apart if they didn't get their way and the men would have temper tantrums that could terrorize the family. When such conditions prevail for long the marriage is bound to crash on the rocks.

The mystery of weak people marrying strong people is intriguing, to say the least. Why does a big wheel on campus marry the school introvert? It's the old story of opposites attracting. If the strong partner married a strong person, how would the one continue to feel strong? Don't you see that the capable person thinks he needs a weak partner to make him feel big and important? Without someone in his life to whom he can feel superior, without someone to whom he can give advice, to lead and guide, he feels inferior. He is threatened by her growth, her independence. It changes his whole life, or so he thinks. (Of course, the same pattern holds if the strong partner happens to be the female.) For convenience only, let's use the example of the strong male and the dependent female.

As long as she continues to grow *somewhat* everything is fine. This growth is allowed, however, only as long as she still needs him. Should her growth get to the point where she begins not to need him, the trouble begins. He then has to undermine her growth so she won't pass him by. She must not get a job, or go back to school, or go bowling with the girls and have a few drinks later. Her role in life (as he sees it) is for her to stay home, take care of the kids, and not mind if he has an exciting life at his job, meeting people and doing interesting things.

This problem does not get corrected until the strong mate learns to relax and not require weakness in exchange for love.

SEX

Of the 215 marital complaints from my study, surprisingly enough, only 26 stated that sex was the foremost problem in the marriage. Again, please bear in mind that disrupted sexual relationships existed in a great many more of the couples I counseled, but in only 26 instances was it specifically the problem causing them to seek help. (Infidelity is listed as a sexual problem when the person was driven into the arms of a lover because of poor and unsatisfying sexual relationships with the mate.) There were five subheadings under the sex category:

Insufficient sex—his complaint	7
Insufficient sex—her complaint	4
He is unfaithful	10
She is unfaithful	1
Impotency and frigidity	4

When the husband feels frustrated over his sexual expectations it usually has to do with his wife's feelings of being rejected in many areas of her daily life. She cannot give of herself erotically in the evening when, as one of my irate clients told me, "the old grouch wants suddenly to turn on the charm for you know what."

It actually surprises me that so many men do not realize that sex for women is often vastly more than the sex act itself. It is that total feeling she has for her mate at the time of intercourse which determines if she will respond to him with passion. That is why a woman can be a torrid sex bomb one night and an iceberg the next. It all depends on what she feels *totally* about her mate. If the feeling is right in the kitchen, it'll be right in the bedroom.

Instead of trying to seduce his wife into being more loving, many men do what comes so naturally to men: blow their tops! The old boy knows well enough he's not getting Brownie points by dragging her into the bedroom by the hair, but he does it anyway. When anger takes over, reason flies out the window.

Eventually he gives up trying to be nice to her and seeks his loving elsewhere.

When a woman feels unfulfilled sexually it is often for several reasons: (1) her husband is simply ignoring her desires for affection out of spite, because he has a low sex drive, or because he's distracted, (2) she is unable to experience an orgasm or (3) he ejaculates too quickly. This leaves her in a periodic state of sexual frustration. After trying to work this out for months or years, the female often gets the urge to step out on her husband, not so much to find someone who loves her, but rather to find out once and for all if she is in fact a totally frigid woman. If her lover is able to give her orgasms repeatedly, she can rightly point to her sexual problem with her husband as the result of poor technique on his part, or bad vibrations between the two. Without her affair she would never have been sure that she wasn't totally the faulty partner. (This is not an endorsement for an affair, it is an objective observation I have made numerous times from my practice.)

One woman resorted to infidelity as a solution to her deteriorating marriage. In a letter to me she describes how she wants to restore her marriage, but cannot let her guard down enough to reunite herself emotionally with her mate. She reached a point of almost no return in her affections.

Dear Dr. Hauck:

Things around here had been rather pleasant up until a few weeks ago. Something has happened to me that I can't explain but still has caused a distance between Jake and myself. I just find it very difficult to warm up to him like I used to and even more difficult to say "I love you" and be convincing.

I don't know—I feel so hollow. I want to be as warm as I used to be but there is something holding me back. The "once burned twice shy" theory would apply, although I would imagine there to be more to it than that. Jake has been trying so hard to please me and still—I feel very little toward our love life. I really don't want to lose him but I honestly can't help this weird feeling I get when he reaches for me. It's a sick sort of feeling.

It's from situations like this that an affair grows. Can you sense how there may be no return to their former loving relationship no matter how much Jake tries? Even counseling is powerless at times to awaken a feeling of hope and love when this point of no return has been reached. The repentant mate can do a 180-degree about-face on behavior that seemed rigid as concrete and still it may not melt the injured heart of the hurt and angry partner.

When it has worked, the party who wanted to save the marriage had to tolerate living with an iceberg for months at a time. Only the charm and tenderness turned on for many months induced the divorce-minded partner to give the marriage a new lease. But what really has amazed me (and the couples) is the complete change that can come over a person who is certain the marriage is over. Women who have been childishly dependent, whining, and tearful marsh-mallows all their lives can snap out of this habit literally overnight. A man I once counseled for months for his unreasonable anger snapped out of that pattern the day his wife moved out to divorce him. To get her back, he amazed her with flowers, conversation, words of passion and endearment, and almost complete control of his fresh mouth, ugly looks, and temper tantrums. You almost have to witness this to believe it.

COMPANIONSHIP

Companionship was the fifth largest group of complaints in the couples I counseled. Their frustrations were of two kinds: (1) "He works too much and we don't have enough time together." (2) "We aren't able to communicate."

The young couple, eager to make ends meet, may feel compelled to have the husband work two jobs. The young mother, with several young children to care for all day, will find it hard to have enough time to nourish a relationship. One of the reasons Holly-wood people have numerous divorces is due to their frequent and long absences from each other. If you don't give each other ade-

55

quate time, all the things that need to be said never get said. Soon the lovers go along their separate ways, meeting briefly for mealtimes and bedtimes.

When the wife, for example, hounds her husband for more of his time, he becomes short-tempered and wants to avoid her nagging rather than give her more company. Becoming more desperate, she puts on more pressure, becomes less pleasant to be with, and drives him farther away. The result is that a loneliness enters into one of the partners at least, an emptiness that was precisely what many marriages were made to avoid. An intimate relationship is still one of the most satisfying of all human conditions. When it's missing, it may not be the end of the world but it's serious nonetheless.

If the loneliness is caused by job pressures or child-care requirements, the couple has to make some concessions be they ever so slight until they outgrow those problems. They could live on less money if he quits moonlighting. She can be taken out at least once a week even if it is for hamburgers and coffee.

If the loneliness is caused by one mate selfishly doing his or her thing while the other holds down the fort, assertion training will be called for.

Poor communication happens when a person is afraid to speak because of an expected ear-chewing or a flood of tears, or when the mate is one of these shy persons who simply does not talk much no matter what.

In the first instance, counseling is often necessary to train people not to fear the rejection of displeasing a mate. Whether your mate gets mad or depressed over your actions, you are not responsible for those neurotic reactions. You are not guilty of another's fury or blue moods. Say what you think is fair and try to do it in a courteous way. If your spouse can't take it, advise professional help.

If your spouse is a hermit at heart, you've got an entirely different set of problems. Some people don't communicate because they are shy and always have been. One woman, in the company of her husband, made this complaint in front of me, hoping I could persuade him to act in a more friendly way. I tried to engage him in a conversation but walked smack into a brick wall. He said,

56

"Nope," "Yup," and "Maybe." That was all. He wasn't being mean or difficult. He was just one of those tall, silent types you hear of from time to time.

What do you do with closemouthed mates? Love them or leave them. You aren't likely to make big changes except on rare occasions. But with some pressures, especially by insisting he take you out regularly, and by having people in to play cards and have coffee, he may be drawn out enough to make life with him comfortable if not exactly stimulating.

Are you wondering why these people complain years after the wedding day about qualities they surely must have seen in their mates while courting? I've wondered about this too and inquired of many clients. They invariably report that they were too in love to let it matter. Furthermore, they fully expected the mate to grow more open after marriage.

FAMILY

Twenty-four people stated family difficulties as the major reason for marital unhappiness. The complaints have the following breakdown:

Disagreement over child-rearing	11
Conflict with in-laws	9
Boredom with motherhood	3
Mate neglected the child	1

The first item, disagreement over child-rearing, can be serious and persistent. If the parents are not united in their rearing policies, the most serious consequences can result to the child.

Confusion over what is right and wrong is one of the byproducts of this condition. Dad lets the boy get by without cleaning his room. Mom pesters him constantly. They get into repeated arguments over why he won't make his son mind and she's accused of trying to make a girl of the boy. The bitterness that can build up between a couple over their children can bring on the worst feelings imaginable. The day comes when they resent being married and especially the day they had children. I have seen dozens of marriages that would have been wonderful if it had not been for the disagreements over the children.

One woman wound up in the state hospital several times because she couldn't get her husband's help in controlling the children. The boy was in repeated trouble in school, the girl was on drugs and earned the money for the habit by prostitution. The mother was desperate to stop this destruction but got no support from her mate. She never forgave him and when she got enough confidence in herself from counseling she left him. Both children were out of the home by then, but she was so disgusted with her husband that his presence was intolerable.

Children are great at using the split between their parents as a way of getting what they want. Though they do not enjoy or plan on the family falling apart, the youngsters find it too tempting to ignore the opportunity to play one parent against the other if it means Joe can borrow Dad's car tonight or Sue can go to a movie instead of study.

If such marriages are to survive, the parents will have to unite in their discipline. Even if you don't like what your mate is doing with the kids, give in if you can tolerate it at all. Maybe he or she will give in to you next time. But when you're alone with the children you have the right to handle them as you see fit. When he comes home and wants to take over with different rules, back away if he disagrees with you. Then, next day, after he goes to work, do as you feel inclined.

Can this confuse the kids? Not as much as you would think. Children, and adults too for that matter, can shape their behavior rather easily according to what is expected of them. I came across the situation a number of times when a child is impossible at home but a model student in school. A father can have his children accepting one set of standards during the evenings and weekends, and a mother can have them mind different rules during the day.

Those couples who have seldom had discipline problems with their children prior to their becoming teen-agers may get the shock of their lives when that age is reached. The most annoying transformations take place in the sweetest and most cooperative kids in the world. That lovable daughter who never gave you a cross word since her birth suddenly takes it into her head to come home when she likes, not to get off the phone when you ask patiently after fifteen minutes, or to cuss you to your face. Mom and Dad often see this transformation differently and want to discipline it differently. That's when the marriage can get into trouble.

The second largest group of complaints in the category of family problems was conflict with in-laws. This subject and the other two: boredom with motherhood and child neglect, will not be further dealt with. They are important, to be sure, but not as important as the topics already covered.

NEUROTIC BEHAVIOR

Neurotic behavior accounted for the marriage problems of fifteen of my clients. Whoever said it takes two to tango was ignoring the fact that some people can cause trouble in a marriage all by themselves. This is an important point to bear in mind because a lot of work in family therapy is currently emphasizing the point that persons become disturbed *only* in relation to other persons. That's why so much emphasis is placed on treating the whole family, not just the person the family labeled as "the sick one." And this often makes good sense. However, I believe it is not uncommon that once a person becomes disturbed in one relationship, perhaps in childhood, he can later enter a series of fine and stable attachments and start all kinds of neurotic trouble. This is because he has a bushel of bad personality habits, and not because of the behavior of anyone else. This is an example of doing the tango all by oneself.

Take the case of Ted. He blamed himself since childhood for not being able to prevent his baby sister from being killed in an auto accident. From then on, every ten years or thereabouts, he would get into real trouble. He encouraged a woman to divorce her husband when he was thirty by making her pregnant. At forty, he was ready for another divorce by impregnating another girl. At fifty, he divorced his third wife because he—guess what? Each time he repeated this plot he lost everything he had and it would take ten years to reach a point of happiness which his guilt had to destroy.

Now how can a girl fight someone with an instinct for defeat that repeats itself like the seven-year locust? This man is destined to hurt himself regardless of what his wife does. He tangos by himself at ten-year intervals. To help him, a therapist would have to get him to understand his guilt, not his wife.

Poor self-discipline is one of those neurotic habits which can cause trouble for your mate. The wife who can't lose weight, keep the house clean, or follow through on disciplining the children can be such a pain to a disciplined husband that friction is bound to develop.

Some of my clients were seriously irritated over the sloppy, careless, and negligent ways of their spouses. Others were ready to climb the walls because their mates were perfectionists. These characters are fussbudgets. They correct people on tiny faults because they make a big thing out of nothing. John is forever yelling at May because she stands before the open refrigerator door, wondering what to have for supper. He also snaps off lights all around the house, turns down the heat at night, refuses to throw out a spoonful of leftovers, and of all the people in the home, he sharpens the pencils. He's a practical fellow but he's intense. That can be as annoying to live with as a sloppy and careless clod.

Alcoholism accounted for one third of those people who were suffering from neurotic marriages. These men had difficulty tolerating frustrations and relied upon their wives to give them moral support. The wives seemed to need weak husbands so that they, the women, could feel important to their men. As long as this pattern didn't get too far out of balance, the marriage could prosper. Sometimes, however, he becomes too demanding, too irresponsible, too intolerable until she no longer cares for her feeling of being needed. That's when they come to counseling.

Chapter 4

How Does a Marriage Really Work?

Let us now examine in some detail the inner workings of most, if not all, marriages. With over two decades of counseling experience I believe that I can speak with some knowledge on this subject.

Marriage, as I've already pointed out, is a business arrangement. The couple need not be in love to form such a company but things usually go better if the partners are deeply attached to each other. I further insist that this arrangement can prosper so long as both partners get a reasonable amount of satisfaction from the business. If the man wants a sexy wife whom he can show off to the world while his wife wants money, power, and an indulgent life, it is perfectly possible for them to be happy even though he is repeatedly knocking himself out for her. As long as she can make him feel proud, he's getting what he wants from the marriage. As long as she is pampered and indulged, she is getting what she wants. Even though her contribution is 10 percent compared to her husband's 90 percent, the two can be enormously happy. Granted, one must be a bit desperate and neurotic to accept those terms, and granted this kind of arrangement is rare. I use it nevertheless to illustrate that such marriages will work according to my theory because each has expectations that are being met by the marriage. When that happens you have a successful and happy marriage. I also maintain that love flourishes when this balance is achieved, because love is that feeling you have for someone who satisfies your needs and deepest wishes.

To understand how a marriage really works, you will want to note these two ideas: (1) love is getting what you strongly want and

(2) marriage is a legal partnership to assure the continuation of those benefits. When something goes wrong in the marriage we must return to these two basic ideas to understand what happened and to discover what can be done to restore harmony.

THE RATIONALIZATIONS THAT PREVENT CHANGE

A marriage in trouble is a marriage that needs to change. That's more easily said than done. The phony excuses people make for not confronting their mates or forcing more benefits to come their way are as numerous as bees around the honeypot.

1. The fear of rejection from displeasing your mate is probably the most frequent excuse for turning into a coward. People are so utterly hung up on being loved practically all the time that they give in on almost all contested issues. They believe rejection hurts, and believing this literally, they avoid confrontations like some boys avoid soap.

What they need to learn is that rejection is unpleasant perhaps, but not painful *unless they let it be.* Only then will it hurt. Instead of having it out with the spouse and risking immediate unpleasantness for the sake of long-range gain, these rationalizers shake like lambs before wolves at the mere thought of suggesting a change. If they do not speak up for their rights every ònce in a while, they will find several unhappy things happening. First, they hate their mates for allowing an impossible situation to continue. Secondly, they hate the marriage just like they'd hate their jobs if the jobs didn't satisfy them. And thirdly, they may even hate themselves, especially because they are gutless and know it.

Resist such rationalizations as: "I don't dare stand up to my mate because I'll get rejected, and I couldn't stand that." More often than you realize you will win in the long run. Decide what you think is your right, tell your spouse what you plan to do if you don't get your way, and then stand aside to avoid the blast. Your lover will proceed to do everything he or she can to get you to accept the *status quo.* But if you are patient and tolerate the rejection for days, weeks, or even months, eventually you'll win (if you aren't divorced) because none of your mate's strategies, schemes, plans, or techniques will have worked.

I was able to diagnose Bertha as a depressive the moment she walked into my office. She had red eyes, didn't smile, spoke softly, and lacked that snap in her walk that goes with confidence and good health. She was a typically dominated wife. She stayed at home while her husband wined and dined with business associates. She wasn't getting much out of her marriage except loneliness, drudgery, and a full-time baby-sitting job.

Bertha gave as the reason for not pressing Bob to be more considerate that he would get angry if she displeased him and not love her until she apologized. Under my urging sweet Bertha reconsidered the awfulness of not being loved and decided to stand her ground.

Bertha soon went out with her girl friends to bowl, to dinner, or to the movies, and Bob had the jealous fit we predicted. She became tense but I had prepared her for that and more. Soon it came. Bob got mad and pushed her around. She left the house that night for a motel (much to his amazement). Bertha was feeling her oats now and could sense the way the game was played. When they clashed again Bob packed his bags and moved out. She was truly upset but tried not to show it. I had warned her that this was the moment of truth. She had to risk losing the marriage by pressuring him for those benefits so important to her. If he couldn't tolerate her expectations, then it was just as well that he leave and she start life afresh in the hope of finding someone with whom she could be happy.

Bob came home the next night fully realizing for the first time that Bertha was absolutely determined to have her way in certain respects and that if he wanted the marriage to continue (he did), he would have to give in to her. Bob tried talking things over with Bertha as he had often done until two in the morning. I cautioned her against falling into this ploy. She was to cut off such talk. Either he was back to accept her terms or he could leave. There was nothing to discuss. Fortunately it worked out well in her favor and because it made her happier she liked her husband and her marriage all the more. This made him happier too.

2. Another common rationalization is to insist that a change will upset your mate so much you'll feel guilty over the pain you caused. This is really too bad because you are never responsible for

the emotions your mate is having. If you displease your spouse and this indirectly causes him or her to be upset, don't hold yourself responsible. You cannot upset people unless they allow it. It is what people *say to themselves* over what you do that upsets them, not what you do.

Mary feels guilty when she rejects her husband's sexual advances. He gets angry, pouts, and withdraws for two or three days, punishing her with rejection and silence. She needn't feel guilty because she isn't upsetting Toby, she's merely frustrating him. *He is disturbing himself* over the frustration she is giving him and he blames her for what he's doing. It is his angry and self-pitying thoughts that are upsetting him, such as: "How can she deny me? She's a bad person for being so selfish. I'll show her, the wench. She'll feel sorry for not giving me what I want."

With these kinds of thoughts running through his head he's bound to be upset. If Mary accepts his neurotic thinking, she'll blame herself for what he's doing to himself. All she needs to do to see that he is his own worst enemy is to realize that he could say mature things to himself such as: "So my wife doesn't want to sleep with me tonight, so what? It's hardly the end of the world. If I continue to treat her kindly, I'll probably be able to interest her in sex more frequently. In the meantime I'll simply have to tolerate these frustrations. I don't have to have my way at any time. I'm a big boy now."

If Toby were to talk to himself like this, you can be certain that it would literally be impossible for him to be upset. Therefore, whether your mate gets upset or not does not depend on what you do but rather on what your mate says to himself or herself *over* what you do. If your spouse doesn't accept that, however, and still insists that it's all your fault that he's upset, tell him quietly and firmly that you're sorry he's upset and you sincerely hope he does something about the regrettable way he makes himself miserable. Perhaps he should go into counseling. Surely there must be a psychologist in the community who can help him with his problem.

That is putting the responsibility for a disturbance where it belongs. Don't cave in the next time you get the guilt treatment from your mate. Read this section to him or her and get yourself off the hook.

3. "I won't be able to support myself. That's why I have to put up with things as they are." Financial insecurity scares a great many women and makes real cowards of them. They picture themselves cast onto the streets, in rags, begging for a living. They reason that it is far easier to tolerate being yelled at, putting up with his drinking, beatings, and infidelity, than to be on one's own.

The great disaster that supposedly takes place with women who are cut off from their husband's purse strings seldom takes place. They usually are able to find work. Or they get support from their parents until they can get on their feet. Perhaps they have to accept welfare for a time. Then, too, the courts are often successful in making husbands pay child support. And lastly, after a couple of years, a new man may enter the woman's life and give her greater love and security than ever before.

Most of the women whom I have counseled and who decided to separate, money be damned, regretted only that it was necessary. If it had to be done, it was better to be a divorced person, making it largely on her own, open for new experiences, than to be the old scared wife who feared life so much she accepted ridiculous abuse instead.

4. Fear of physical injury is enough to quiet some women. They have seen their immature husbands rant and rage and all but foam at the mouth while they growl angry and dirty words at their frightened mates. They have often seen them smash furniture as though it were made of matchsticks.

It's not unreasonable to suppose that a husband might turn that violence on his wife if she stepped out of line. I concede that. But should that ever happen, I'll give you the same answer I've given other women. Strike back, defend yourself, even if you have to do it violently. No one has the right to impose his will forcefully on you. You wouldn't for a moment accept such behavior from the seediest bum on the street. Why accept it from your mate?

If you need to arrest him to protect your body and life, do so. If you honestly think he's psychotic or weird, hospitalize him. Don't make your phone calls in front of him of course. Wait until you have privacy. Then, if you must, pack a bag, dig up some of the money you've saved for this occasion, and call a cab or get in your car and spend the next day or so in a motel. When he's apprehended and cooled down, talk with him. If he's sorry, good. Perhaps you can try to work things out. If he threatens to kill you, tell the police and tell him you told them. Also assure him that you have no intention of being his punching bag again ever. Should he try it again, tell him you'll bring criminal charges against him.

This is tough talk, I know. But I honestly cannot advise otherwise. If you have been socked around, you have that problem because you acted weakly in the past. Tyrants take advantage of weak people. If you want your husband's respect, don't put up with his inconsiderateness.

5. "I don't want to upset the children by standing up to my mate and I certainly don't want to ruin their lives with a divorce." This sentiment is honestly expressed by men as well as women. Nothing is so stressful to children as watching the two most important persons in their lives act like snarling baboons. If you back away from your spouse to spare them this anguish, I applaud you. However, suppose your sacrifice doesn't achieve what you want it to achieve. What are you supposed to do then?

Look at it this way. If it seems to you that you are so unhappy that some change has to occur, then don't sacrifice yourself too long. If you do, you teach your children how to knuckle under to bullies and that running from a fight is mature behavior. You do them no service if this is what they learn in the family. Therefore, if a reasonable amount of asserting yourself does not cure the friction, rather than go on endlessly subjecting your children to these neurotic scenes, leave your mate if you can. If a ship is sinking, you might as well save yourself and as many others as you can.

Can children be raised well with only one parent? Of course they can, often better than with two quarreling parents. Kids can adjust, if given time. The weekends spent with the separated spouse can then be more enjoyed than ever his or her company was while the family was united. So fear not. If your marriage needs adjusting, don't delay. Don't use your children as a rationalization for not standing up for yourself. If worse comes to worst, the separation isn't as bad at times as keeping the family together.

"Don't Look a Gift Horse in the Mouth"

I worked with Georgia for months, trying to get her a more equal arrangement in her marriage. She was a most dutiful wife, kept her husband's meals hot long into the evening if he was late, made his weekends easy by doing the yard chores herself, and let him make the major decisions. She was unsure of herself when she fought for her own needs and felt guilty and selfish when she occasionally won out in a dispute.

Over the months, however, she did indeed grow in fortitude, became more of an adult wife than an obedient child bride, and it looked like marriage counseling was about to make some neat changes in her relationship with Bobby, her husband.

Wrong. Things began to go backward again much to my surprise. I asked Georgia about this and she wasn't able at first to put her finger on the heart of the matter. In her next session though she brought out the source of the trouble.

"Bobby is making changes, all right," she reported, "but I feel he's doing them merely to please me, not because he's convinced I'm being fair."

"So what?" I asked.

"Well, who wants changes from a husband who thinks he's being abused when he makes concessions?"

"Anybody, I hope," was my instant reply.

"Honestly? Wouldn't it bother you if you knew concessions were made grudgingly, not with a cooperative and willing spirit?"

"I suppose I'd always prefer to have people go along with me cheerfully but that's expecting too much from life for one thing, and secondly, it's irrelevant."

"Irrelevant? What's so irrelevant about my husband just doing me favors under pressure?"

Georgia's dilemma is not uncommon. If you've been troubled by it, consider the following argument.

1. Don't expect to win a popularity contest when you press for your rights at the bargaining table. All change involves frustration and no one enjoys being frustrated. Therefore, if you can't tolerate

getting some advantage at the price of frustrating someone else, keep your complaints to yourself.

2. Why can't you accept benefits from others even though they're given grudgingly? In other aspects of your life you do this with the greatest of ease. When you get a raise, for instance, do you actually suppose for one moment that most employers are happy to pay out more money? They may feel you deserve the raise but it wouldn't break their hearts if you were content with less. On the contrary, you feel you're entitled to more and whether the boss likes it or not. You're usually self-interested enough to ignore that fact.

3. It is important that your mate learn to share in the benefits of marriage. If he or she is not accustomed to decent give-and-take, then start now to teach how to be frustrated gracefully. How do you do that? Obviously you frustrate your mate over and over again until he or she learns the act of compromise. Unless you do that you'll merely miss a fine opportunity to teach your partner how to share and then you'll be putting up with the same old injustices you've tolerated in the past.

4. Lastly, if you're really fair in your complaints, chances are you will eventually be happier in your marriage even though you had to go through a period of mild rejection. Nothing pleases one mate more than the knowledge that the other mate is happy because of his or her efforts. By sticking to her guns and not caving in, Georgia became a much happier wife and in a short time Bobby didn't mind making his sacrifices. He was becoming a happier husband.

The old saying "Don't look a gift horse in the mouth" is still saying a mouthful.

We needn't explore all the reasons why people shy away from change. The important point to bear in mind is that some marriages are miserable and in need of changes but for one unacceptable reason after another nothing much happens. I want to share a surefire method that gets results more often than anything you've tried before.

ONE DEED IS WORTH A THOUSAND QUARRELS

When you are frustrated by your mate to the point where you feel compelled to lessen that frustration, your first strategy is to talk over the matter to see if you can get a compromise. If that fails, you have two choices: back off and accept the situation as it is, or try another tactic. Let it not be words any longer, let it be action. Goethe, the famous German poet, put it nicely: "Thinking is easy, action is difficult; to act in accordance with one's thoughts is the most difficult thing in the world."

Watch how this works. A client once reeled off to me a list of things she asked her husband to do. He meant well but never got around to fixing the fence, repairing the closet light, and fixing the kitchen sink. On several occasions she threatened to call in a repairman, but his protest at paying someone else for work he could do in a few hours was so heated she backed off and merely wept at the frustration. When she became depressed over putting a pan under the kitchen radiator to catch the water from the leaking pipe and doing this for over six months, she came in tears to see me. My response to her was immediate: I pushed the phone to her, asked her the name of her plumber, looked it up in the yellow pages, and had her make an appointment with the man as soon as possible. I told her not to say anything to her husband when she got home that night. He didn't deserve the courtesy. When the work was finished she could give him the bill.

Would he raise the roof? Of course he would. So what? How many times would he get bent out of shape over that matter once he made the initial complaint? Even if he kept it up, that would still be less frustrating in the long run than putting up with the leaky pipe. And lastly, she would be teaching him that if he didn't act, she would. And that is the point of the lesson.

If you want your mate to change, change yourself first. Frequently you have your problems with domination because you permitted it. How? By using one or more of the rationalizations I've listed above.

Do differences between the sexes always have to end up in a battle of the sexes? Obviously not. If compromises can be reached,

69

well and good. It is when neither side is willing to negotiate that a man and a woman are wise to do precisely what labor and management do: strike. How long? As long as your determination holds out. Furthermore I predict the spouse who cares *least* for the marriage will usually win the strike. That's ironic and regrettable about the human condition perhaps, but it is true by my observations.

The mate who is most indifferent to the marriage is willing to risk divorce more readily than the mate is who will do anything under the sun to preserve it. Take the case of a married man who sometimes had lunch with females in the adjacent office. His wife was furious over this but he, feeling fairly secure, and not willing to pay just any price for wedded bliss refused to eat with the boys every weekday. His wife threatened divorce but he was prepared for that too. If that's what she wanted, she could have it, he told her. At this point she realized that he had the bigger lever. She either had to give in or lose a marriage that meant more to her than to him.

Sometimes you can be fooled by this bold talk about not needing the marriage, as Karl and Debbie found out. He was very unhappy with her management of the house and children. On many occasions he tried to get her to act more responsibly but her answer was always, "If you don't like it here, don't let the door hit you in the rear as you leave."

Brave talk, and it seemed genuine also. Karl got his fill of the problem one day, however, and decided to divorce her. Much to his shock and utter amazement, she became tearful, got on her knees, asked for another chance, and finally took an overdose of pills. Karl waited until she recovered and then left for good.

How can you tell whether a spouse is really indifferent or only acting that way? You can't. You'll have to make your move as Karl did and watch what happens. How regrettable it is that our verbal warnings are often so ineffective. Action, on the other hand, is unmistakable. Having lunch with people your spouse is jealous of is an undeniable fact. The *act* of having lunch says everything while your *saying* you will have lunch with them says nothing.

The best way to communicate is through deeds. Try words first, to be sure. But don't spend years screaming at each other. Words are too easily misunderstood to make really good communication. But deeds—that's an entirely different matter. _Doing_ something about your frustrations instead of just _complaining_ about them is one of the most important habits each mate can develop.

WHEN TALK IS _NOT_ CHEAP

I have repeatedly emphasized the need to rely on deeds, not words, to make yourself understood. There are a few exceptions, however, and one in particular is extremely important.

Men, but women especially, want to be _told_ they are loved. They don't want it suggested, hinted, alluded to, or demonstrated in a thousand ways. They want to hear you _say_ it. The words "I love you" must come from your lips.

The way they are said is important too. They had better be said with sincerity or the whole thing can become offensive. They don't need to be said in moments of passion necessarily. In fact, women often object to husbands who can say them only during lovemaking.

"I love you" wants to express a spontaneous thought, a feeling that is suddenly so strong it can only be expressed with words. It had better be said periodically rather than once every ice age or your mate will ask you, "Do you love me?" and your answer may be, "Sure," or "Of course I do." That's not likely to lead to trouble from a few such inquiries, but unless you pick up the clues she's giving, she may feel increasingly threatened by her need to ask for assurances. The more she asks if she's loved, the less she feels loved. Sadly, the more reassurance she asks for, the less he's inclined to give. "Give me time," he insists. She counters with, "If once in a while you tell me you love me, I wouldn't ask."

Why is it so hard to some men to say these important words to the person who means the most to them of all the people in the world? Men are not raised to be poets. That's considered anti-masculine. Getting mushy, tender (romantic in other words), is to act like a sissy. That's not true of course but he can't fight his childhood conditioning. To be sentimental is to become weak, it's like inviting castration. What red-blooded male is going to stand for that?

Instead, he's a realist and spurns mere words to show his loyalty and affection. Some men put it this way to their wives, "Telling you I love you doesn't mean a damn thing." By this they mean that actions speak louder than words and that sweet talk can't make up for a man working hard for his family. They go by the motto, "The proof of the pudding is in the eating." They want to show love, not by words, but by service and devotion. If he brings home his paycheck regularly, doesn't stay out late, invites the wife along on his trips, supports her the best he can, if he does all these things, isn't he showing his love?

Of course he is, who would deny it? Then why does he still have to be forced into the difficult role of the romantic? Because, gentlemen, it is necessary, that's all. You may knock yourself out servicing your mate, but she can't be certain you are doing those things with pleasure, with gladness, and that you don't resent her. You could, after all, sacrifice for your family and not love them. That's why the verbal reassurance is so important.

Look at it this way. If you were given one raise after the other and if you were promoted three times in one year but no one ever told you how well you were doing, wouldn't you miss the praise? You might think a pat on the back, an expression of appreciation or admiration were not needed in view of your career success, but let's face it, the whole business would be infinitely sweeter if you were toasted at the dinner table that night, if you got a phone call from a friend congratulating you, and if the company sent you a short letter of encouragement.

That's when talk is *not* cheap.

HOW SELFISH DO YOU WANT TO BE?

One of the quickest ways to ruin a marriage is to let your mate have his or her way on important issues most of the time. If you do that, I accuse you of not protecting your own interests in the marriage. It is virtually important to the success of your relationship that you fight for your rights to the point where you can say comfortably: "I like this marriage now. I get my way just enough that I feel contented and happy more often than I feel unhappy." If your mate can say the same, the marriage is on sound footing. Each spouse is selfishly looking out for his and her own interests to the point where the marriage is a satisfactory relationship. I feel it is your responsibility to make yourself happy in your marriage. It is not your mate's job, it is yours. Look out for those benefits most important to you and (1) compromise on them, (2) stand pat on them, or (3) give in fully this time but bargain for your getting your way fully next time. Remember, marriage is a business the purpose of which is to *make you happy.* If it is not doing that, the fault is largely yours because you are afraid, or feel guilty for wanting your personal needs and desires satisfied.

Recently I counseled a woman who was depressed because she was on the verge of her third divorce. She was able to analyze her problem quite clearly. May was always reluctant to stand up for her rights. So she allowed her mates to have their way time after time. As the months and years rolled by she gradually developed a strong and conscious feeling of bitterness against her husbands. This led to a distance between them, sexual coldness, quarrels over a hundred little and irrelevant issues, and eventually to her seeking a divorce.

Had May asserted herself much earlier in the game and risked rejection over minor irritations, she would have *protected* her interests. Having done that, she would have been more content with herself, her mate, and the marriage. By looking out for herself to a *reasonable degree,* she would have saved her marriage.

If you want a good marriage, see to it that you enjoy it. If not, you will eventually quit, just like you'd quit any job that was turning sour on you. Frustrate your mate *a little now,* instead of *greatly later.* When you come right down to it, the fastest and best way to destroy a marriage is to give in to your mate all the time because you think pleasing the other person in every way will ensure the love you seek. I wish it were so. Ever hear of being taken advantage of? Too often that's what happens. The honeymoon is almost over when you feel your partner is getting a lot out of you but you aren't getting much in return.

The Cold War

All right. Let's suppose you assert yourself. What happens then? First of all you can expect a protest. It usually comes in the form of complaining, pouting, quarreling, or even a physical pushing around. Things are really going to get bad. But never mind. You can't make omelets without cracking eggs.

When talk doesn't bring you around to be the sweet and generous character you used to be, your mate will begin to act. A man may start drinking, staying out late, not bringing home the money. A woman will let the house go, prepare the meals late or poorly, and maybe run up bills. Neither partner may feel especially sexy at these times, so their love lives suffer significantly.

You are now in that phase which I call the cold war. How long it will last and who will win depends entirely on how important your cause is and how much you're willing to sacrifice for it. I advise you, however, to sit tight. Let the storm rage. Remind yourself the worst that can happen is that you may get a divorce, something that may well have happened anyway. Your chances of saving the marriage actually *go up* when you act like a strong person who is willing to stand up for your rights. When your mate learns to respect you through such acts as self-assertion, you'll find that you'll be more loved also. I've found that it is very difficult to love someone you don't respect. The only exceptions are children, aging parents, or the mentally impaired. We seem able to love individuals in those categories whether we respect them first or not. The average adult, however, must earn love through being respected. A doormat is not an object of respect, therefore it cannot be loved. It's that simple.

Your partner will proceed with a series of maneuvers, or strategies, calculated to get you to be the nice and compliant person you once were. You will be accused of always getting your way when you know you give in 90 percent of the time. There will be concerted effort to make you feel guilty by acting hurt and blaming it on you. This is emotional blackmail. "If you keep doing what you're doing, I'll get so depressed I'll have to be hospitalized again," is the overt message. The silent message is, "I hope you feel so guilty that your conscience chokes you, you dog."

In addition to these tactics there is physical abuse, infidelity, or threats of divorce or suicide. This phase of the cold war can last days but sometimes stretches out to years.

It's a tough period during which the weak spouse usually caves in. Two events tend to give the suffering mate the strength to resist. First, the school of hard knocks eventually teaches you something. You remember what you had to contend with in the past and you resolve you will not put up with it again.

Secondly, counseling, and the learning of some of the insights that come with counseling, teaches you *(a)* not to be so afraid of rejection and *(b)* that you never need to feel guilty over frustrating your mate. If you understand both of these principles, you'll be strengthened to stand against the unreasonable demands of your mate.

Then comes the time of waiting. The cold war can be long and frigid. Give yourself six to twelve months after you've made it clear you want big changes in the marriage. Tell your spouse he or she has that much time to shape up or someone will ship out. Don't make idle threats about this. Do it if you threaten to do it.

Don't be so afraid to take a stand that will make lots of waves for a while. It usually is not as awful or devastating as you imagine. Most of the time you'll win if you stick to your guns. Surprised? I can certainly understand why. The arguments get so heated you don't think you have a ghost of a chance to win. Stay with it. More times than not you'll eventually win the day if you fail to give in as the cold war intensifies.

Tony was one of those sweet and easygoing fellows who was doomed to be henpecked. Angela didn't care much for lovemaking but she did care about money. She owned the house and the business (both from her first husband), and handled all finances. Tony insisted that he have an equal hand in all these matters and that's when the cold war started. Her first strategy was to scream at Tony. Then she became sarcastic, called him a half-wit, an ungrateful slob, etc. When this did not move Tony she tried talking to him nicely, made love frequently, and tried in general to seduce him. I prepared him for such tactics so he was able to accept her love overtures without giving in.

Her next move was more desperate. She promised a divorce if he persisted in telling her how the family inheritance would be handled. Tony gulped but told her the choice was hers: either she brought him into the business as an equal partner or he'd leave her. This was the final test. She did not back down.

Now Tony had to decide which way he'd go: stay or divorce her. He left. But at least things came to a head and allowed him to see just how unimportant he was. That was important for him to realize. The process took several months. Years later Tony phoned to say he had remarried and was quite happy this time.

In the past, his dread of the cold war and his inability to prepare himself for one strategy after the other would have weakened him in no time and left the problem worse than before.

I have seen people try to manipulate their mates with neurotic behavior so intense they had to be hospitalized. From their hospital beds they'd give out the message: "See what you did? If it hadn't been for you, I wouldn't have taken an overdose or driven recklessly." Do not fall for this ploy. Your wedding vows are not a jail sentence. You have a right to happiness also, and unless you're willing to face the artillery barrage your mate throws at you the moment you decide to become uncooperative, you've had it.

WHAT RIGHTS DO YOU HAVE IN MARRIAGE?

Most people haven't the foggiest notion of what they're entitled to as a partner in their business. Below is a list of some of the more important expectations which if not met cause friction.

1. Companionship: You married for it most likely. So when your spouse buries his nose in a book all evening, or becomes hypnotized before a television set, you have the right to complain. You were drawn to your mate as a friend. Real lovers are also great friends. This item is so important that those of you who are engaged to doctors, salesmen, or pilots, and the like had better think about the many days you will be lonely or else you'll feel cheated on this very important element of a happy marriage.

2. Sex: You shouldn't have to go weeks and months without intercourse. You could have done that without marrying. And you have the right to expect the *way* you have sex to be satisfying at

least some of the time. If you prefer morning lovemaking but your mate prefers the evenings, the usual give-and-take will solve the problem. If one of you wants to sleep with pajamas while the other likes to sleep in the nude, press for your wishes *some* of the time and be prepared to give in at other times.

3. Growth: More important than sex is your right to develop your personality and abilities as you see fit. If it's important for you to be an artist, you have the right to pursue that interest. Your mate is wrong to put you down or not grant you time for your artistic development. Do you want to go to college and finish your education? Do it. You have the right to expand your horizons even if your mate is threatened by your growth.

4. Maturity: You have the right to expect (not demand) reasonably mature behavior in your spouse. It is not your responsibility to spend your life making him or her happy at the cost of making yourself miserable. Your mate has the responsibility to look out for his or her own happiness and to see to it that important desires are fulfilled without always requiring your presence. If she, for example, is a wallflower at social gatherings, she has no right to expect you to be one also. Her problem is her responsibility. She had better do something to overcome her shyness instead of insisting *you* always do something to make her happy. If she has no desire to grow or change, why should you make efforts in her behalf that she won't even make?

5. Privacy: Some people need to be alone. If this is your style, face it. Teach your mate to accept some degree of separateness from you. This means you may want to read in your room an hour each evening, go on separate vacations occasionally, or just go out walking by yourself. Some people won't understand this hermitlike pursuit, but so be it.

6. Freedom from slavery: This may sound strange in a book on love and marriage but actually it is quite appropriate. Slavery means someone owns you: your body and life are not your own but belong to your mate. Tragically some marriages are hardly more than contracts between a master and a slave. A man can easily believe he owns his wife no less than he owns his car. After marrying her and supporting her he believes he has the right to make her stay home, have sex, indulge him, dance with others when he

permits, and go out in the evening to a movie or a club meeting if it suits him. The same insanity can happen when a woman thinks she owns her husband and can control his life as though he were her slave.

You have the moral right to personal dignity and freedom. You are a slave to no one, and marriage does not make you one. The marriage vow of love and devotion certainly never meant you were to be possessed like a piece of furniture.

Healthy couples understand this without being told. They know always that their mates are with them by choice and by choice they can leave. When you don't like working for a particular business it only makes sense to leave if that will substantially improve your situation. If your boss forbade you to leave, you'd think he was completely unreasonable to suggest he owned you. But sometimes in marriage this basic right to freedom is ignored and unrecognized, permitting slavery to continue between two people who started out wanting love.

The most frequent complaint of couples who sought marriage counseling was being dominated by angry and controlling spouses. That's what slavery actually is. It is domination by angry and controlling people, nothing less. Small wonder it turned out to be such a significant complaint. Nobody owns you body and soul, unless you permit it. If you do, may the ghost of Simon Legree visit you in your nightmares.

7. A fair share of the family income: If you are the wage earner, stop thinking that the paycheck is yours because you brought it home. In a partnership both parties are entitled to a share of the profits.

In cases where the husband is the sole wage earner, the wife has agreed to give up working outside the home, but she did not give up working. Homemaking, housekeeping, and child-rearing are work and any man who doubts it should give it a try. Had the wife decided to get a job, she would have been independently secure. Now that she has removed herself from the job market and gone into the marriage partnership, it's only fair that she should have a voice in managing the family finances and a share of the income as well.

78

A Case Study

The following is a transcript of an initial therapy session with the wife of a man I saw the previous week. I cite it here because it touches on many of the points I have discussed. She was married for five years and separated from her husband for six months. The client lost the feeling of companionship because of poor communication and a great deal of loneliness.

THERAPIST: Why did all this happen? You say you have lost your feeling of love for your husband. Is that right?

CLIENT: Yes. I lost it because I just didn't have him around to fulfill my happiness and my loneliness that was going on inside of me.

T: What were you looking for from him?

C: Companionship, communication, love, understanding, just being around me, just being my husband.

T: And he couldn't do that because—

C: He had his mind occupied with selling and he was gone a lot. When he was home he usually had to do a lot of paper work, which I understood. I understand that part of it. That was his business but I wanted half of that too.

T: Do you have any children?

C: No children.

T: So there weren't even children to take up the slack when he left. You were all by yourself. Were you working at the time?

C: I've been working for about six years. That's what I did. I started putting myself into my career, boosting myself more and getting more involved. I'm an interior decorator. I started going to classes this past year. It was hard for him to accept that because when he was home maybe on the weekend perhaps I would go to a class and he wouldn't accept that. He couldn't understand it. He didn't want me dedicating my time to my work when he was home and that started a lot of friction. I had to get out. I had to find myself. I had to see what was going on inside of myself. And I have and I'm happy. It's not because I don't have him. I've never had him because I've been by myself for so long.

T: I sense you felt guilty for taking off and leaving him and you didn't know whether that was right.

C: Yes. He didn't want it. He didn't want me to do it at all. But I had to. I thought about it for six months and I finally started talking to him about it. I told him what I was going to do to kind of condition him to it. He didn't want me to do it at all. He wanted me to stay there with him and still does. But I've got to find that love for him again before I go back to that same situation.

T: What would he have to do in order for you to feel loving toward him again? What must he do for you?

C: I don't know. I really don't know. I don't love him anymore. I've lost it.

T: Do you know why?

C: Because I didn't have him.

T: What does that mean, "You didn't have him"? He was there. He was providing for you and he still loved you all the time he was driving around the state. You knew all that.

C: Well, I wasn't sure. I thought he did but I wasn't always sure of that feeling. I don't know what he could do for me. I just think it's all in myself. I think I have to help myself before he can do anything for me. We sat down and talked a lot and he is willing to do just about anything for me. But I don't want it that way. I want him to be himself because I am myself.

T: No you don't. You see, that's the point. You didn't want him to be himself before. You wanted him to keep you company. If you really wanted him to be himself, you would have been happy over his being so absorbed in his work. But in four and a half years you were sorely disappointed on that point. As a matter of fact, you were so disappointed that your whole dream died. He didn't fulfill his part of the bargain as you saw it. When somebody doesn't do what is important to you I maintain that the love feeling dies, and you're a good example of it.

C: What do you do?

T: If it isn't too late, he had better give you exactly what he didn't give you before.

C: I feel like it is too late. He has asked me to come back, but I have no desire to do this. We've had some discussions since then about going back to my home, but I don't want to. I have no desire to go back to him again. It's going to be hard for him because he tells me he still loves me and he wants me back and all that. I love him as a human being but I cannot get the feeling back of husband and wife again. I've tried. I really have. I've been giving a lot of me but I just need more time and that may make it even worse.

T: Well, it may do one or the other. It may make you feel like you made the right decision to separate, or it just may give you the feeling that the marriage can be saved. You may enjoy him again if we can get him to do and to understand what is important to you. It died in the first place because certain important expectations on your part were not being fulfilled. If he started to fulfill them today and your feeling isn't totally dead, you might be able to revive a strong feeling again. Then you'd say: "Well, this is more like it. This is what I wanted all along. I loved you because of the fun we had, the companionship we had, the talks we had, all these things, and now it seems maybe you understand that and I'm beginning to feel something for you again."

C: How long do you think that would take?

T: Give yourself from six to twelve months to see just how you feel at the end of that time. You know how long you want to wait. You know how much more of your life you want to invest in this possibility. I think it's wise to wait. If he can rekindle the old flame, you'll be glad you waited. If at the end of that time it doesn't seem to work out, then you can always tell yourself: "Well, all right, I'm going to separate with a clean conscience. I did my best. I wasn't hasty. I saw a professional counselor. I gave it all the time I possibly could and it just really hasn't worked. I have fallen out of love. I just don't care that much for this man anymore and I am leaving." And that is a fair decision. He has no gripes coming at that point. But I don't want you to feel guilty about falling out of love.

C: He didn't make me feel that way intentionally. I have hurt him.

T: How?

C: Because I don't love him anymore.

T: Well, that doesn't hurt his feelings. He hurts himself.

C: How's that?

T: He hurts himself when you don't love him. Granted that's

very easy to do, but you don't need to feel guilty because he's depressed. He distresses *himself* over the fact that you no longer love him. That comes from his saying certain depressing things to himself like: "Poor me. Here I am, losing my lovely wife for whom I care so much. I can't stand those changes in my life. I find this whole thing regrettable, and I am very sorry for it," and so on. When he talks like that to himself he's bound to get depressed because he's blaming himself and also because he feels sorry for himself.

C: Is there any way I can help him? I feel like I should. It's like he lost his best friend because that's what we were at one time. And then we just lost that too. I feel like I've let him down in all different aspects. I don't want to let him down that hard. I feel like a creep.

T: You feel like a creep because you are separating and letting this man down. Is that it? Okay. Let me again explain. You went into the relationship in the very first place expecting certain benefits to you. Right?

C: Yes.

T: You expected financial security, love, tenderness, attention, companionship, sexual fulfillment, maybe a family, protection of some kind, all these things. In a sense you set up a business, as I call it. The name of the business is Marriage, Inc., or Mr. and Mrs. Smith & Company. And you hired him to do specific things for you. He is an employee of yours. He is a partner in a business. Suppose you opened up a business, let's say a dress shop, and you hired this person to do certain things and he didn't do them. What would you do?

C: Fire him.

T: Yes. Would you feel guilty about it?

C: No.

T: Why not?

C: Because it would be the right thing to do if things weren't balancing out the right way.

T: Exactly. In other words if the business isn't working out, you simply don't feel guilty about it, you may feel regretful that it had to happen but you don't say, "I'm a heel because I'm getting out of the business."

We want to see whether there is time to correct this employee's behavior toward you. He didn't understand some of the things that were necessary to make this business run. He thought all he had to do was work hard and come home and give you a paycheck and that's what was expected of him. He didn't understand the other obligations. You are making that very clear to him now, aren't you?

C: Yes.

T: Okay. Let's see whether he can fulfill those other obligations. If he can, you may say to yourself: "Hey, I am not going to fire this employee. I'm not going to divorce my husband, because I think he is coming around. He is beginning to understand why I hired him in the first place." But if he doesn't start shaping up in terms of satisfying some very fundamental things in your relationship, then you have every right to say: "Look, you and I just aren't getting along. You don't give me what is important to me. I can't love anybody who doesn't treat me well." You see you only love people *after* they do nice things for you. And he wasn't doing nice things for you. That is why you fell out of love. If he does nice things for you again, satisfies your deepest desires and some of your needs, you may then begin to love him again. Follow me?

C: Yes, but I'm not attracted to him anymore and that's making it difficult for me.

T: Yes, maybe you're at a point of no return. I don't think anyone knows this for sure. That's why I say you may want to give it six months to a year to really check it out and make sure that this whole thing cannot be revived again. I can talk to him and try to show him what you are disappointed about and what he has to do to get you back. Let's see whether he can pull it off and whether your feelings might be changed. If they can, beautiful! If they can't, well, then, regrettably you may have to go your way. Does that make sense?

C: Yes. I'm not sure I want to make this happen and that's making it difficult.

T: Yes, I know. In other words, you're not quite sure you want to go through six or twelve months of—

C: Well, I could probably, in spite of myself, go twelve months or whatever. To make sure, maybe I do need more time, I don't know. But right now, I am very strong about how I feel. And I know what I want and what I don't want. Maybe it's the independence that I have had that has made me feel this way. I don't know. I am happy the way I am living now. Before I was a married single girl.

T: That's right.

C: And now I'm still married but I'm on my own.

T: Is there another man in the picture?

C: No. I have friends but I'm not ready emotionally for another relationship at all.

T: Okay. I hope you understood the one point I was trying to make. When you marry someone you have the right to expect certain things. Do you understand? And if you don't get them, your contract is not being fulfilled.

C: Should I leave him then?

T: Give yourself six to twelve months. Okay?

C: Okay.

Chapter 5
Living with
Your Neurotic Mate

We are all neurotic from time to time. The real task of making a marriage work is coping with your mate when he or she is disturbed. It's easy enough to get along with your partner when he's a sweetheart and she's a dear. That takes little talent. If you're not frustrated and you're getting your way 99 percent of the time, why shouldn't your marriage run smoothly? The test comes when there is conflict, when your spouse acts flaky, unreasonable, suspicious, ungrateful, or just plain weird. To deal with that nightmare, you need to understand several important psychological facts.

Neurotics act neurotically. They can't help being selfish, domineering, spoiled, or mean because that's what it means to be neurotic. Disturbed people can't act like normal people when they're frustrated. If they could, they wouldn't be neurotic. Therefore, don't be surprised if your wife, who has an enormous inferiority complex, turns purple when you compliment her friend's dress. She has to do that because she's insecure, and insecure people act that way toward everybody. If you were taken out of the picture and Mr. X took your place, in three weeks' time she'd be feeling the same way toward him. You don't need to take her behavior personally since it has nothing to do directly with you. It is part of her neurotic makeup at that time.

Instead of getting bent out of shape over her nuttiness, try to change it if you can. If you can't, accept it philosophically. What else can you sensibly do? You could get all upset yourself, but then you'd be adding another neurotic to the situation and that's hardly what you or she needs.

A middle-aged client asked me what he could do about his wife's constant hostility toward the children. She made it so unpleasant for them that as soon as they were able each left home. Jealousy of the husband's easygoing style with his children plus her resentment of the demands of motherhood were part of the reason for her problem.

His response to her was to get angry, depressed, and confused. She wouldn't consider counseling, so what could he do?

My first piece of advice was not get angry. She had a right (a neurotic right) to be a selfish and mean mother. She probably didn't like being disturbed any more than they did, but until she could learn how she talked herself into those moods there was no way she could actually stop being disturbed. He and the children were advised to predict and expect dumb actions from her because she was neurotic.

"But she's not dumb," he protested.

"Right. But her actions are," I reminded him. "Forgive her and accept her as a poor upset human being who never learned how to be kind or how to accept herself or others as mistake-making mortals."

"I could forgive her for some of the stuff she does, doctor, but honestly, she's so unfair in her attacks at times that I just can't overlook them."

"Yes you can," I insisted. "If I showed you an X-ray of your wife's brain right now and could point to a big dark area that meant she had a tumor in the brain, would that change your attitude toward her?"

"Of course it would," he assured me immediately. "With a tumor on the brain she wouldn't be able to control her thinking or feelings to a normal degree."

"True. Now, if you can accept crazy and unfair behavior from her if she has a physical tumor, why can't you accept it if she has an emotional tumor, so to speak? One is as crippling as the other."

"I get your point. You're suggesting I wouldn't like her behavior in either case but I could always tolerate it and not blame her for it."

He got the point even more fully when I suggested that he would not be surprised if his wife fell once in a while, injured herself, and even broke the furniture if she had epilepsy. Epileptics do that. To insist epileptics *shouldn't* do that is to demand that epileptics not have seizures. Impossible (unless it is controlled by medication, of course).

To live with a neurotic spouse, therefore, make up your mind not to insist on a change in his or her disturbed behavior. *You* change instead, by talking yourself out of your grandiose demandingness and *then* see if you can help your mate.

ANGER—THE WORST PROBLEM IN MARRIAGE

If you can accept the idea that when frustrated, disturbed people have no alternative but to show their disturbances, you will automatically spare yourself the worst problem you can have in marriage: anger. Nothing is as dangerous to a relationship, in my opinion, as anger.

Briefly, the psychology of anger is this: you talk yourself into anger *over* the problems your mate gives you. First you wish, desire, or prefer you would get your way (more sex, respect, or responsibility). Then, without realizing it, you change those healthy wishes into neurotic demands by saying, "I *must* have more sex." "You *ought* to give me more respect." "You *should* take more responsibility." When you use demand words such as "should, ought, must, and have to," you are doomed to anger if your mate does not comply. If, however, you did not make demands but kept them wishes, desires, or preferences, then if you were frustrated, you would not be angry, you'd be only *disappointed* and *regretful.* Whether you become angry or not, therefore, depends not on what others do, but on whether you have been making demands.

Does this sound a bit fanciful? In practice of course. No one is so rational that he can control his thinking all the time. No one is perfect. In principle, however, my statement is true and would actually be demonstrated if we weren't such error-prone people.

Frank is an example of the power anger has to ruin a good relationship. It seems he had been turned on by some of the new sex literature on the market. Since his own sex life was so dreary he began to resent his wife's puritanical ways after learning how

87

great sex can be to some people. He wanted to seek out prostitutes so he could get some of the thrills he fantasized and which his rigid wife was not about to satisfy.

Although she was a good woman, loyal and hardworking, she had many prohibitions about sex. He couldn't keep a sex manual on the shelf with the rest of the books. Open discussion on sex was frowned upon and sex was permitted only for having children. Thinking herself a proper lady, she never made a single sexual advance in all the forty years they were married. As Frank put it bitterly, "Sex for joy seemed unattainable in our marriage." His deep anger was expressed in wanting to experience wild orgies with ladies of the street.

Frank believed that his wife was making him angry. I insisted that this was not true, even though he was seriously frustrated by her for forty years. *He* was disturbing himself by childishly insisting that he *had* to have sex his way and that she had no rights to be puritanical and unexciting sexually. She had every right to think that sex is only for procreation, that all sex literature is filth, that discussions of sex are evil, and that a lady never makes a pass at a man. Frank and I agreed completely that she was dead wrong on every issue. Still, she has the *right to be wrong*. People who have had bad sexual experiences, or who have been taught all their lives that sex is bad do what Frank's wife did. They can't help it. It's their problem in life and their cross to bear.

For forty years Frank was sexually frustrated and bitter and resentful as well. Anyone who has to put up with the one problem (a sexless spouse) certainly doesn't need another (anger), particularly when it's of his own making. Frank's anger led him to several other problems. He felt guilty over it, and then would suppress it. His wife never really heard his full reasoned views on sex and therefore never had her neurotic attitudes challenged. Furthermore, instead of nursing his resentment, he would have been far better off looking for a solution to his frustrations. This he seldom did because he was anger-focused, not goal-focused. And lastly, his suppressed rage turned him into a sourpuss. Because he found it difficult to be nice to her, she found it difficult to be nice to him. For forty years neither yielded an inch.

The most frequent complaint of over two hundred clients seeking help for their marriages was a dominating and angry husband. This was given by forty-one persons as the major reason for their unhappiness. When I point out therefore that anger is the most dangerous condition for a marriage I feel quite justified. No matter how tough the frustrations are, you make things worse if you get *chronically* angry. Occasional anger may be healthy for a marriage even though you are upsetting yourself for a while. It clears the air. However, more than occasional anger is never recommended. If you can remain a firm person and manage your marriage without violent scenes at all, you have reached maturity.

A man complained to me of his neurotic wife. She was an extremely frustrating person. As long as her children were small and obeyed her she was fine. When they became teen-agers and began to think for themselves she hit the ceiling. No one was going to challenge *her*. She was always right. Anyone who didn't know that (her husband included) was just dense. It was wrong to question her, and those who thought otherwise could pack their bags. The husband was accused of being a sex maniac when he showed any kindness to his ten-year-old daughter.

Inevitably he developed a dangerously high blood pressure, so intense was his anger. However, as justified as his anger sounds, he was still wrong for having it. His wife was clearly a troubled person and as such could not behave differently. Disturbed people act like disturbed people. They aren't patient, mature, unthreatened, polite, or sensible. They're defensive, thin-skinned, impulsive, and hard to live with. If they could behave any differently, they wouldn't be neurotic.

The husband became angry because he demanded that she not be neurotic. Of what use is ordering another human being to be sensible? His big mistake was in converting his *desire* to have a loving wife and sweet mother for his children into the *demand* that she straighten up and fly right. Whoever gave him that authority, pray tell?

So what choice did he have? He could have held his peace by accepting her as a disturbed person. He could have pressured her into changing by setting a good example, even if he had to go into counseling himself. Perhaps he could have learned to be kind but firm (not angry). And, failing all these, he could have left her and fought for custody of the children. Lastly, he could have become chronically angry and compounded his troubles.

Let's face it, loving a grouchy and mean person has got to be the most charitable act of the century. You simply can't get close to someone who is always finding fault with you or never agreeing to those simple pleasures which make life beautiful. You married in the first place because you wanted certain services from your mate. But if he or she is the angry type, can't you see how you're bound to be unhappy? Angry people have to have *their* way all the time, so where do you come in? You loved that person because of what he or she was going to do for *you*. If that person is easily angered, however, that means you're supposed to do all the giving and ignore your own needs. Presto! You won't get what you want because you don't count.

One of the best ways to deal with an angry mate is to rid yourself of your own anger first, and then be kind and considerate. The worse your mate is, the nicer you'll want to be. Frankly, it's quite difficult continuing to be angry at someone who is answering your emotional upheavals in a kindly way.

You may be wondering if this advice to be extra sweet won't wind up in your giving in all the time with you eventually being dominated. True, that's a distinct possibility, but only if you confuse kindness and considerateness with agreement. You can deny and disagree with your mate, and you can still do this in a polite and considerate way. You certainly don't need to be weak just because you're not angry. Stick up for your views in an unemotional but firm manner. If you do this for months at a time, it's the rare mate who won't change somewhat. Remember, the worse he or she is, the nicer (but firmer) you'll want to be.

THREE WAYS TO HANDLE AN ACCUSATION

Unfair accusations rank among the most frequent causes of emotional upheaval, especially in marriages. Unless you know how to handle these, you're doomed to endless screaming matches.

If your mate accuses you of being stingy, immediately ask yourself two questions: Is the statement true? or Is it false? Think it over carefully before deciding. But if you conclude the statement is true,

90

you have two more questions to ask: Do I mind being stingy? or Don't I mind?

If it troubles you to be a tightwad and you think you have been tightfisted lately, don't hit the roof because someone has pointed that out to you. Instead, tell your mate: "Thanks for telling me how cheap I've been lately. Only someone who cared about me would risk making such a remark. I don't want to be unreasonable with my money, so I'll really watch it from now on."

Furthermore, just because the accusation is true is no reason why you need to feel guilty or depressed. So you have a few big faults. Doesn't everyone? Aren't you human? Do not judge yourself by this one aspect of your behavior. Instead of hating yourself and spending a lot of time blaming yourself, think of what you want to do about your problem.

Now consider the second possibility: the accusation is true but you don't think it's a fault. In short, you agree that you're tight with money but also consider frugality a virtue. So why get angry because your spouse has touched on one of your paramount qualities even if the revelation was meant as a slam?

We tend to forget that we may be quite pleased with a habit until someone complains about it. That makes us wonder if at times there isn't something wrong with us. That's what Lew did. His wife accused him of being overprotective of his mother. At first he was quite defensive because he felt attacked. Later he had to agree that he was very attentive to her, but that was perfectly okay with him. Lew felt obligated to her for the many kindnesses she had always shown him. He felt good about spoiling her at times. She did it for him numerous times during his upbringing and it didn't hurt him in the long run. So his wife thought he was indulging his mother and he couldn't completely disagree. "But since when did a little indulgence kill anyone?" was his philosophical response.

The third strategy you use to keep from getting angry over an accusation is to decide that the protest is false. You are not stingy. You have, in fact, been generous beyond expectation. You have denied yourself time and again and hardly expected such an unkind accusation. How, under these circumstances, do you remain calm?

By giving your spouse the right to be wrong. By accepting the fact that she has the right to her opinion that you're cheap and indulgent, you protect yourself against an inner fury that could tear your marriage apart. If the accusation is wrong, it's wrong. Why get disturbed over another's shortcomings?

This can literally apply to any false accusation. If someone accuses you of being a Communist, a homosexual, or a drunk, don't take it personally. Either you are or you aren't. And if you aren't, smile at your accuser and say: "You may be right, but I think not. However, to each his own."

This advice, if you follow it closely, can actually be the difference between harmony or hatred in almost any relationship.

JEALOUSY

Some people think it's cute to see their mates green with envy. It supposedly signifies a deep and lasting love, a most flattering expression of care and devotion. Perhaps so, but according to my experience jealousy is like tabasco sauce: only a drop of it is necessary to get the desired effect.

Chronic jealousy is a wicked and extremely destructive problem that can do nothing less than cause a serious split between the couple.

When your husband won't agree to let you go shopping because you took the liberty to see some friends without his permission, you'll then see how cute it is to be loved in this neurotic way.

When you're a few minutes late from bowling and he gives you the third degree as to whom you've been seeing, you begin to get the taste of a nightmare.

When your wife gets depressed because you spoke to Miss Curves at the Christmas party, watch out! She'll have a lot more to say when you show normal courtesies even to her friends.

Jealousy in any degree is a pain in the neck and every marriage is better off without it. What causes this green-eyed monster? Your own inferiority feelings. That's right. When you tell your mate how jealous you are, you're admitting that in your own mind you're worthless and insecure.

Here's how the psychology of jealousy works. You are threatened by the possible loss of your spouse's love because you have no confidence in yourself. You think every Tom, Dick, and Harry

92

or every Sally, Rosie, and Jane can beat your time. How little you must think of yourself if you're frightened you'll lose out to everyone! And this can even include parents and children.

If you had real self-respect, a good feeling about yourself as a person, it simply would not occur to you to get so threatened by others. "What do they have that I haven't?" you would ask yourself. "Even if they do take my mate from me, I'm still desirable enough to find another mate. So why worry?" That's what the secure person says.

Should you attempt to quiet your jealous mate's worries and endlessly answer questions as though you deserved the third degree? No, at least not more than once or twice. Beyond giving these polite assurances, however, don't say a word. There is no way you can satisfy such questions except by admitting your guilt. You can deny all day that you didn't sleep with someone else but you'll never be believed. Your mate is waiting for only one answer, that you were unfaithful. *That* answer will be believed in a minute. When your spouse hits the ceiling because you're not responding with the expected answer, suggest that counseling be sought to take care of the jealousy problem and to get off your back.

SEX

Though sex is one of the strongest drives we have, it is also one of the most subject to neurotic complications. Failure to have an orgasm is among the more common sexual problems in marriage, whether it be the male or the female. In the male this problem is called impotency, in the female, frigidity. I don't like those labels because they suggest a condition that is irreversible: once frigid always frigid, so to speak. Nothing could be farther from the truth. Unless a person has something wrong physically, orgasmic difficulties usually result from fear of failing again, from guilt over trying to enjoy sex, or from distracting problems.

Tony was a full-blooded American male, virile all his life, a roaring bull in bed, and a charming fellow. Something happened one day at the shop which shook his confidence. He was passed over for a promotion by someone whom he trained. He took it on the chin in front of the boys, but deep in his heart he was crushed.

93

Shortly thereafter he was unable to maintain an erection long enough to satisfy his wife. Then things got even worse, until he was unable even to begin. That scared him enough to seek sex counseling.

I diagnosed Tony's problem easily and quickly. He was thinking about the disgrace at work so often that he didn't forget it when he made love. Thinking about a missed promotion is hardly sexual thinking, and that's what it takes to do a complete job of intercourse. He had to be taught how to distract himself from his problems, leave them in the shop, and concentrate on lustful and sexy images when he closed his bedroom door.

Sex images are just that: thoughts of your mate's body (the shape, the smell, the touching) spiced with love talk. If your mind isn't on that kind of thinking, you're not likely to get charged up.

Tony insisted, however, that he *was* thinking sex all the time he was with his wife. His erection was on his mind constantly. That's what he meant when he insisted that he had sex on his mind all the time. Actually he wasn't focused on sex at all. He was thinking of how *awful* it would be if he failed his wife again. He thought of what a neurotic and unmanly character he'd be if he couldn't satisfy her soon. And lastly, he began to wonder if he was a latent homosexual. This he was calling sexy thinking. It was nothing of the kind. These thoughts would turn him on about as much as a cold shower would.

I emphasized over and over again that he was a normal male, that he could satisfy his wife again if he'd stop thinking of the shop, the promotion, and the supposed humiliation he received. He was not even to entertain the possibility of losing his erection again. Instead, he was instructed to think of those parts of his wife's body and those actions which would excite him. He was practically guaranteed to succeed if he did that correctly. If he didn't make so much of succeeding, he'd relax and do much better.

This is more easily said than done, however. Luckily there is another solution. In the event Tony couldn't maintain an erection, he was instructed to fondle his wife to orgasm. He literally didn't need a penis at all. There are other ways to get an orgasm and there is no reason why they should be ignored. Additionally, if he knew he was not going to frustrate his wife's sexual desires, he then was

94

less likely to worry over his own performance. He did indeed improve until he was back to normal.

We must get over the idea that intercourse is the only way men and women can satisfy each other. It's a great method but not the only one. Tony managed a good sex life for a time without having a good functioning penis. Women too can have a full and satisfying sex life without intercourse.

Many women simply cannot have an orgasm by intercourse. They always require special and additional stimulation. Perhaps the nerve endings in the vaginal area are weak, or perhaps other faults exist. In any event, women who cannot have climaxes from intercourse sometimes panic and go on a promiscuous spree, jumping from one bed to the next in search for that one perfect organ that is going to give them an orgasm the normal way.

Relax. Women too may simply try too hard and worry too much, obliterating those delicious thoughts during intercourse which normally bring on a climax. Think whatever it takes to get turned on. Go ahead and dream of your favorite movie star instead of your husband. Don't feel guilty. (That's not sexy, remember?) If you have success often enough by thinking of past boyfriends or movie idols, the day usually comes when you'll be getting so much enjoyment from your mate that thoughts of him alone may be all that is needed to bring orgasm.

Forget about impotency and frigidity. Those words can scare the passion right out of you. Just consider yourself undergoing a period of great distraction from worries or guilt and nothing more. If you get back on the track and think pleasurable thoughts while making love, you'll find your ability to reach orgasm returns very nicely. If you've never reached orgasm, even after following the above instructions, you may have to conclude that you're one of those millions of women who require additional fondling. And what's wrong with that?

Occasionally a person will wonder about the possibility of the mate's being homosexual. He or she then becomes frightened and wonders what to do if the mate really is a homosexual.

This is another bugaboo that needlessly disrupts the sex lives of married people. First, stop and realize that everyone is capable of homosexual behavior. The most honest people are fully capable of cheating, lying, or stealing. Yet we hardly brand them as *criminals* if they get a bit careless with their morals from time to time. We simply talk to them, point out our objections, notify them of possible consequences if such behavior continues and wait to see how the objectionable behavior is modified.

It's the same with homosexual behavior. Suppose your husband is showing excessive attention to a male friend. Let's further suppose his sexual interests in you have been going down lately. You might correctly conclude that this *normal, heterosexual* male is choosing for a time to practice homosexual behavior, which he is perfectly *capable of avoiding* if he wishes. So you'll talk to him, protest, and warn him that you won't stay married if there is infidelity with anyone, female *or* male. Then the choice is up to him.

In rare instances some homosexual men and women seem so driven to seek partners of their own sex that genetic and physical factors, not psychological factors, seem to be operating. In a great many cases, however, homosexual behavior is consciously chosen. Therefore it can be consciously modified just as readily.

Helping Your Mate Be Neurotic

If your husband or wife has been depressed, angry, nervous, jealous, or poorly self-disciplined for some years, consider the distinct possibility that you may unwittingly be encouraging that neurotic behavior. You may complain bitterly that he does not pick up his clothes. If that problem has been going on for more than several months, the chances are that you have taught him to leave them lying around. Odd, isn't it? You can't stand to act like his chambermaid, but without realizing it you may be making it easier and easier for him to drop his clothes wherever he undresses.

How? By picking them up. You see, he listens with his eyes to what you do rather than with his ears to what you say. As long as you keep telling him how you hate to pick up dirty clothes but pick them up anyway, why should he change? You are training him to drop his pants wherever he disrobes. He probably wouldn't do it unless you rewarded him for letting them rest where he undressed.

This pattern can become rather complex and then it really gets interesting. Take Joe and Fran. When he's irritated with her housekeeping he yells at her and compares her to her immaculate and perfectionistic sister. He does this because he has found over many years that she really feels the sting of his comments if he yells and if he makes comparisons. Now how did he find this out? By seeing her get angry, and flinging herself across her bed in a shower of tears. When she did that he let up.

In other words she trained him to yell at her because she didn't react *until* he yelled. He trained her to throw herself onto the bed in a crying rage by making up with her the moment she did. The yelling was being rewarded and so was the crying. Can you see why they had been doing that for years?

If everyone compliments you on the length of your hair, the chances are that this will seem so rewarding to you that you won't change the hairstyle. Behavior that is rewarded is strengthened, even neurotic behavior.

We do this all the time in our families. When you ask your child to remove the dishes and she doesn't, you probably repeat the request. After the third request you yell angrily. Then she jumps up and does her chore. What has happened? Your first inclination is to say you've trained your girl. True. But to what?

On closer inspection you will see that you have gotten off her back only after you yelled. You trained her to wait for the yelling before she knew you meant it. The next time you want to give her an order she probably won't respond until you get sore, because nothing happens until you yell. If you penalized her calmly after the first request, she wouldn't wait for the third command which you have to give at the top of your lungs.

She, however, has trained you too. Only when you finally get angry at her does she move. That means she is controlling you by rewarding you with acceptable behavior only after you yell. The yelling pays off—she sees to it that it does. Therefore, whenever you want action out of her you'll remember that yelling worked well before, so it'll work again.

Have you ever wondered why people take advantage of you, why they walk all over you? Hold onto your doormat! You train them to deal with you like that because you give into them when they boss you. If they get what they want by being bossy, why should they change?

This means that you must study your actions carefully when you are repeatedly in a state of upheaval with another person. Chances are that the two of you are training each other to act neurotically and you don't even realize it.

IS HONESTY ALWAYS THE BEST POLICY?

Under most circumstances I'd say "Yes" to this question. This presumes, however, that your partner has gained reasonable maturity and is not so fragile that the truth would be seriously upsetting. After all, isn't open communication one of those important ingredients psychologists have been saying all along would make for a happy marriage? And hasn't it further been stressed that if you don't tell the truth, your mate's trust in you could be lost forever?

Still I insist that this had better be done only with people who can take the truth. To be completely honest with some persons is like giving a baby razor blades. Consider what you face if your fragile mate asks you if you ever regretted being married. If you have entertained such thoughts and your mate has a low self-image, I can assure you that you have opened a can of worms. It would obviously be foolhardy to be perfectly candid with such an individual.

Look at it this way. Would you offer someone shrimps who was allergic to them? Would you try to get your friend drunk if you knew he had to drive home soon? Would you let your son drive your car if you knew he was too inexperienced? I doubt it. For the same reason I suggest that telling the truth to people who are incapable of dealing with it had better be spared if at all possible.

Does this mean that you are wrong to approach your mate with important matters if you suspect beforehand that he or she will be upset? That would be unrealistic, obviously. For instance, you are absolutely sure you want a divorce. You are also fairly certain your mate might become hysterical or depressed, start drinking, or perhaps even attempt suicide, if you made that decision known. Are you being moral to confront your mate? My view is: yes, you are being moral to stand your ground and speak the complete truth, even if he or she later gets so disturbed that hospitalization or psychotherapy is required. When an issue is extremely important to your welfare, don't let the neurotic reactions of others hold you back. You don't need to feel guilty over their disturbances because you haven't created them, they have. This even applies to attempted suicide. That's right, you don't drive others to such desperate measures. They do that by themselves.

Then when does it make sense to protect your mate from the painful truth? When it does not hurt you to withhold it, and when you believe nothing important is gained if you take him or her into your confidence.

What really does it matter, for example, if you don't tell him you had a serious romance before your marriage? It's none of his business in the first place. But secondly, if he's going to blow a gasket if he finds out about your past, why do it? The responsibility for not hearing this unpleasantness rests with him. If he were less threatened and less neurotic, there would be no problem about speaking out fully.

The next time your mate accuses you of holding back the full truth and tries to put you down for it, simply throw the responsibility back. Inform your spouse that the truth will always be forthcoming the moment he or she demonstrates that the truth is not going to bring on screaming, nagging, crying, accusations, threats, and self-pity. Who needs it?

Chapter 6
What Marriage Counseling Is All About

People in marital trouble are increasingly seeking professional aid to help them with their emotional problems. Many psychotherapists, clinical psychologists, psychiatrists, ministers, and social workers like to work with marriage problems, and some confine their practices to this counseling. Marriage counseling is increasingly recognized as a valuable service to couples who can't see their way out of their conflicts.

When to Seek Marriage Counseling

When you aren't able to bring stability to your marriage by your own efforts, get help. Sometimes it only takes a session or two to give you a new outlook, a new direction. Why stumble along with a manipulating mate for fifteen years when in fifteen minutes a therapist can give you insight as to how you are encouraging your spouse to use you and what you will have to do to bring it to a halt? I mean that. I can give all kinds of valuable knowledge in fifteen minutes.

For example, emotional blackmail is a strategy people use to get their own way. Its aim is to make one feel guilty enough to give in. If you don't understand this technique, it can choke your conscience so badly you'll feel strangled. But when you know what's happening you can be in control of the matter and make things come out for the better.

Jordan, a forty-five-year-old male, used alcohol as his emotional blackmail weapon. If he didn't get his way, he'd get bombed. Then

100

Jordan would get angry and the family got scared. That was just what the old boy wanted. He was blackmailing his family: obey me or I get drunk.

One session with his wife was all that was needed to give her the courage and insight to handle this problem maturely. The next time he terrorized the home, she had him arrested and committed to the state hospital's alcoholic unit. She didn't show him the slightest bit of guilt.

He didn't know what hit him. Naturally he was as furious as a jilted bridegroom. To this she countered by going to the lawyer and drawing up divorce papers. She informed Jordan they would be served on him if he didn't straighten up pronto and no maybes about it. This did wonders for the family. In a short time she learned how to handle his manipulations by not responding to his tactics. Certainly she could have figured that out by herself, but not quickly. Psychotherapy could educate her in a short time to what would otherwise take her years to learn.

The same is true if you are unhappy over your relationships with your parents, or your in-laws, children, sex life, and even finances. In short, if you've tried to bring harmony and peace to your marriage and it hasn't helped, try counseling. If even that doesn't work, you have a conscience free of guilt. You tried your best, knowing you gave the marriage everything you could.

Opening Channels of Communication

One of the strongest reasons for seeking marriage counseling is to get talking again with your spouse, but to do so without the usual hostility that takes place at home. A great many troubled marriages are at such a state of friction that very little is spoken between the couple. They've said over and over again what they feel and it's done nothing but open old wounds. Soon each partner learns that it is easier to go around the house in cold silence than in heated debate.

But that leaves the fundamental issues untouched. To resolve them, it is important to open channels of communication again, but to do so in an atmosphere that encourages quiet discussion. That's where the marriage counselor comes in. Whether the counselor is a clinical psychologist, social worker, minister, or psychiatrist is not as important as is the opportunity the counselor provides for them to discuss their most sensitive subjects.

Counseling gives each spouse a chance to express views from his or her vantage point. If the wife is afraid to criticize her husband at home about his neglect of the children, she may get courage to do it in front of the counselor. He will ask the husband to wait until she has had her say. The husband is then given the same chance. This experience is sometimes new to people who are in the habit of interrupting each other. Their full views are seldom expressed.

With this process operating, people have literally been amazed at what they heard their mates say. For the first time in her life, for example, Betty learned how completely selfish her husband thought she was. He said so during a session with his wife present. He started out by telling her how egocentric she was, something he had started to say many times before. Just as he began his attack, however, she became defensive and blasted him with a reminder of how lazy he was. The result? Neither had a chance to explain in detail what those statements meant.

This time the counselor asked Betty to wait until George had his complete say. George related past grievances Betty had long forgotten but which he still nursed. She was ready to spring at him in defense again but was held off politely by the counselor. George went on and on, elaborating, answering questions by the counselor, until it seemed he had made his point fully.

Then Betty was asked if she wanted him to explain any of his statements. Instead, she proceeded to condemn him angrily. That's the sort of thing that had happened repeatedly in the past and it shut her husband up or brought out a vicious rebuttal.

To avoid this dead end, the counselor reminded her that George wanted only a calm appraisal of his ideas, not a fight over them. In particular, she was asked to say *why* he felt as upset as he did, and *what else* troubled him. At no time just yet was she asked to make a judgment of his views, only to understand them. If she chose to ignore them later, that was her right. For the present, however, it was important merely to learn what the problem was.

Nothing like this occurred between them until a third party

intervened. Because they were mature and socially alert people they did not want to show their worst side to a stranger. That forced them to be civil, which in turn allowed them to communicate better.

Whom Can the Marriage Counselor Believe?

The wife gives one set of details, and later the husband may give another set. So whom do I believe? The answer is: both. I have to assume that each partner is telling me the truth *as he or she sees it.* Truth is often a matter of interpretation and this is especially true in marriage.

She complains he drinks too much. Because her dad was an abusive alcoholic, for her two beers after work means that he's becoming a drunk. On the other hand, he was raised in a family that drank wine with the evening meal and really tipped the jug on family gatherings and holidays. Two beers a night to him was like brushing his teeth, something everyone should do.

The counselor doesn't have to sit between these two people and decide if two beers is too much or not. What the counselor tries to do instead is to get them to make compromises that each can live with, and teach each to put up with whatever frustration remains.

For instance, if the husband is willing to have one beer each night and get home a bit earlier, she might get enough comfort from this to let the matter rest. She won't be completely satisfied, of course, and neither will he. But if they can tolerate that minor discomfort, a temporary resolution to the problem has been reached without the therapist having to decide for one party or the other.

Even if he does not believe one partner, the therapist can still proceed as though he did and come out in the end the same way. If a man told me that his wife was a flirt and she denied it, I'd assume that both were right and then teach each how to live with the problem. He doesn't have to get angry because she has a right to be a tease and if he ignores the matter, he'll calm down soon enough. When talking to her I again can assume that she's right

103

about his unreasonable jealousy and teach her to tolerate his behavior if she can't get him to change. In neither event, however, must I take sides when the versions from each one are totally opposite.

MUST A COUPLE ALWAYS BE COUNSELED TOGETHER?

I know there is wide disagreement over this among counselors. My experience strongly indicates that married people can be counseled separately, together, or even one exclusively and still bring benefits to the relationship. Too many people say, "I would have come for counseling years ago but my husband [or wife] wouldn't come, so I couldn't."

This is a serious mistake. Some mates are so threatened by therapy that snowballs will freeze in hell before they agree to seek help. That effectively removes all counseling from that marriage and the injured party has to wait for years or put on increasing pressure until the spouse gives in.

Instead of following such an unwise course, get the education you need to handle a difficult mate whether or not your mate is willing to cooperate. You have a certain amount of knowledge to soak up, so get to it. It may, in fact, be easier to do this alone—without your mate in the office. Does this mean marriage counseling is not done with the couple together? No, it is usually done with husband and wife together during the same session. However, the notion that good marriage counseling cannot proceed with but one mate is dead wrong.

For example, your mate is socially shy and does not volunteer to go out with other couples or have couples in for dinner. If he or she won't learn to overcome this problem in therapy, what is to prevent you from coming to counseling by yourself to get some pointers on what you might do about this problem? You could, for example, make arrangements to dine out and just take your mate along so often that the fears would eventually lessen. Or you might be taught to assert yourself enough to invite people in even though your mate is lukewarm to the idea. In due time the practice might become more comfortable. To get this courage, you would have to be taught to overcome your guilt for placing your partner in an uncomfortable situation. You would also have to be counseled not

104

to react to the rejection you would probably get. These suggestions would involve you mainly. Couple counseling, as good and appropriate as it is, need not be taken as the only way. Lots of good marriage counseling is achieved by seeing one partner at a time, or only one partner at all.

MARRIAGE COUNSELING AND PSYCHOTHERAPY

The big difference between these two kinds of therapy is that marriage counseling always involves the strained relationship between a husband and a wife, while psychotherapy deals with a person's problems with others from any sector of life, including himself or herself. This means that marriage counseling is one form of psychotherapy just as play therapy with children is a specific form of psychotherapy. The fact that the word "counseling" is used instead of "therapy" is unfortunate because people think it isn't as good, as powerful, or as first-rate as psychotherapy. Actually, giving psychotherapy to a couple is about as difficult a form of therapy as there is with the possible exceptions of treating psychotics or autistic children. To bring harmony into the lives of two persons who are ready to divorce takes skill no beginner can achieve. The marriage counselor is usually mature, preferably married (although this is not essential), and skilled in human dynamics. Some insurance companies don't reimburse the counselor for marriage counseling, but will if it is designated as psychotherapy. Do you see how one label has more prestige than the other?

WHAT CAN I EXPECT FROM MARRIAGE COUNSELING?

You can learn to understand yourself and your spouse better. If changes are needed, you will probably be surprised to learn that you will have to change first. Your mate isn't likely to budge from his or her neurotic habits until you stop making life so comfortable by *tolerating* those habits. To do this, however, you'll need to learn what you've been doing that allowed your spouse to make you miserable. That's the first step. The second step is to learn *how* you can change if you want your partner to change.

For years Mabel apologized for making her husband upset. He

105

was possessive and insecure. She was attractive with an outgoing personality that scared the wits out of him when they socialized. To keep her to himself, he would accuse her of flirting, being boisterous, and thinking she was better than he. Naturally he expected these barrages to upset her so she would be more reserved and thereby give him less cause to be afraid of losing her.

This sad arrangement went on for years until she became increasingly guilty and depressed over the unhappiness she supposedly had caused her husband. Moreover, she wasn't finding living with Bobby all that pleasant anymore. Finally she came to psychotherapy about her depression. To help with the depression, it was necessary to deal with her marriage. Though I never saw the husband or even talked with him on the telephone, I was able to show my client how she let him intimidate her and what she would need to do to alter things.

First I showed her how Bobby was keeping her weak and unsure of herself by attacking her the moment she became confident and self-assured. Each time he jumped on her she felt guilty because she believed that (1) she was upsetting him emotionally and (2) if what he was telling her was really true, she had no right to act as she did.

It simply was not true that she upset him. We cannot upset others. There was no good reason therefore why she needed to hold herself responsible for emotional pains he was giving himself. This helped her to overcome the guilt feelings. If she wasn't actually responsible for the neurotic ways in which he responded to her actions, then what in heaven's name was there to feel guilty about?

At this point things changed. She felt better about herself, was more relaxed in company, and when he attacked her she simply refused to accept the blame. This shocked Bobby because he sensed he had lost an important lever by which he had controlled her. His natural reaction was to become even more angry in the hope that he could scare her back into her old neurotic attitude. Mabel would have none of it. Now the problem with Bobby's insecurity was thrown squarely back into his lap. Gradually he made enough adjustments to become more tolerable to live with.

During this time of his wife's marriage counseling he took a strong dislike to me even though we had never met. It was I, he felt, who was causing his wife to change into a kind of person he did not like, at least for the present. I often find this to be the case. The therapist is seen by the partner who stays out of counseling as an evil character, out to destroy the marriage and cause the client to desert the family. Regrettably, when both partners are not seen personally by the therapist this is a condition that occasionally has to be expected.

The marriage counselor is like a neutral negotiator between labor and management, sometimes being on the husband's side, sometimes the wife's. Above and beyond these little shows of favoritism, however, there is usually a strong interest in preserving the marriage, not only because the counselor thinks that's necessarily a good thing to do but also because the couple are seeing the counselor for that purpose.

What is expected of the marriage counselor if one mate wants a divorce and the other does not?

It all depends on how sound the counselor believes the marriage to be. In most instances the therapist wants to unite the couple. In rare instances, however, the therapist feels that the couple should break up. Some marriages are such sad affairs and such colossal mistakes that it is better to encourage both partners to divorce so they can try marriage again with someone more compatible. It takes courage to break away from a sick marriage and the counselor can sometimes be the catalyst who helps two people escape the neurotic stranglehold they have on each other.

He was a weak and dependent fellow, married to a buzz saw of a woman. A blind man could see that he wanted to get out of her clutches, and he had my backing all the way. His growth depended on being freed of her influence. So I urged him to think for himself, accept her rejection if she decided to punish him, and then decide if he wanted to try to change her, or just leave her. Sure enough, with the aid of some assertion training he began to stand up for himself and she lit into me with full fury. What was I trying to do? Wasn't I a marriage counselor who was supposed to help people stay together? Couldn't I see that he was becoming rude and impossible to live with?

I couldn't get her to see that he was trying to say something very important to her. He wanted more say-so in the relationship if he was to be happy with her. All she could see was his rebellion, not his high goal. She came down on both of us with a determination that made him knuckle under and made us terminate therapy. I never saw him again, not after she whipped him into shape. His high moment was over. Like a skyrocket, he exploded in a brilliant shower of hope only to burn out and leave the darkness behind. Marriage counseling had failed them because they remained together.

There are millions of couples who believe that a divorce always means failure. I don't see it that way. Most people see their marriage as a success only if they remain married until they die. Why should this be? Have two persons failed if, in their close living with each other over many years, they each have the freedom and strength to grow as individuals to the point where their newfound directions lead them apart? Hardly. Would you say that you had failed at a job because you stayed ten years, grew with it, but eventually found it unstimulating and left it for more challenging work? On the contrary, this is advice we give our children and loved ones all the time.

Don't think for a moment that I am advocating divorce for everyone the moment the marriage gets dull. I am suggesting only that divorce need not be viewed as a failure. There are times when it can also be seen as a natural and sensible outgrowth in the lives of people who find themselves trapped in a relationship that offers little hope for fulfillment and happiness.

There are times when a person (in this instance it is usually the woman) wants a divorce but is afraid for financial reasons to leave. If the marriage cannot be saved, the counselor attempts to give her the courage to find a job, borrow money, return to school, or whatever, in an endeavor to make leaving less frightening. I have found that young mothers with several children, little education, and few skills feel locked in their marriages only because they need their husband's pocketbook. They are the love neurotics who are afraid of life and feel constrained to remain in a dependent relationship. When their husbands make life so uncomfortable that they want to leave they suddenly realize they are about as prepared to support themselves as their children would be.

Some will admit outright that they aren't in love anymore and

108

would leave at the drop of a car key. Others will not be that honest with themselves and they may then rationalize: the children need their father; it's wrong to divorce; he's the best I can probably get, so why not be content; I'll never be able to make it alone, etc. Such a wife could be asked: "Would you leave your husband if he decided to molest your daughters and abuse your son, turn the house into a brothel, bring dope addicts home and demand that you sexually satisfy his friends?" The answer is always, "Yes," and from then on she has no defense, for if she can make the break over issues of that severity, can't she make it over her present complaints? If she cannot, she will come to realize that her problems aren't all that bad. The choice is hers to make and she can always make the break if she wants to.

Among my female clients who have opted for divorce but who need training and education first, guilt arises now and again. They believe that they are being immoral to use the marriage for their own vocational benefit until they can get training, find work, and leave. I encourage them not to apologize for their self-interests for the following reasons: (1) They will be less of a burden on their ex-husbands if they get good jobs. (2) The more secure they are financially, the better it will be for the children. (3) As partners in the marriage (Mr. and Mrs. Incorporated), they have every right to a share of the funds coming into the business. Without their numerous contributions as cook, chore girl, baby-sitter, mistress, nurse, gardener, office girl, and traveling companion the men wouldn't have all the cash the women feel so guilty about sharing. Had they decided to work instead of to stay home to care for the house and children, they would have amassed a savings account of their own, progressed in their work, and not needed the men's help now. So, from several valid viewpoints they need feel no guilt because they want to stay married only for financial reasons and leave when they don't need the husband's money any longer.

The most relevant reason why a woman need feel no guilt, however, is that she is only doing what all married people do to each other: use them for their own ends. This is the nature of the marriage relationship, like it or not. It's selfish right from the first date. You marry for specific benefits. If enough benefits exist in the relationship, you get to the point where you can even love your business partner. However it's perfectly possible to run a business without falling in love with the boss and it's perfectly possible to have a civil marriage without love. The young lady in question had better realize that the love in her marriage/business relationship has withered away, but the business is not yet bankrupt, not by a long shot.

WHEN COUNSELING WILL NOT WORK

I've already pointed out that marriage therapy is among the more complex tasks a counselor undertakes. There are a number of conditions that make successful therapy just about impossible. Counseling won't work when:

1. One mate drives too hard a bargain. Most relationships are based on give-and-take to a degree where each is reasonably sattisfied. When one mate gets too hard-nosed, however, there is no compromisng. When that happens the ball game is over.

Bob got the message quite clearly from his wife when he approached her with the following expectations:

1. Spend one evening a week with me.
2. Call me if you're going out after work.
3. Be honest.
4. Have sex once a week at least.
5. Contribute one third of your wages to the family.
6. Discuss any purchases over fifty dollars with me first.
7. Tell me what you dislike about me.
8. Be consistent, firm, and kind with the children and let's agree on discipline.

He handed her this list on a sheet of paper. As reasonable as they might sound to you or me they weren't acceptable to her. Wasn't she clearly telling him that the marriage was over and that any compromise, no matter how fair, would be rejected? Marriage counseling is powerless to reunite two persons who are this far apart. Further counseling was needed for the husband's adjustment to the impending divorce, to be sure, but counseling for the couple was certainly over.

2. Confidence in the counselor is undermined by one of the couple. It's easy to make the therapist look bad by misinterpreting

110

him to the partner. I'll never forget the time I was counseling a very hostile couple. They spent so much of their session time ventilating their angers that I decided to counsel them separately. During one session with the wife I described some of her husband's behavior as "neurotic." I then explained further that neurotic behavior is common to all of us at times. Whenever we get upset and cause ourselves pain, we are acting neurotically.

The next time they quarreled she said he was "a nut" and that "Dr. Hauck said so." The husband was so hurt by this "stab in the back" that he terminated therapy then and there. I didn't learn of this incident until months after they divorced.

Persons in counseling are well advised not to use the therapist as a weapon against the mate. Let the therapist work for both, not for just one. And for heaven's sake, they should not quote the therapist out of context merely to put down the spouse. Everybody loses when trust and confidence in the therapist are lost.

3. The clients are impatient and do not realize the time it sometimes takes to make personality changes. Take the case of the wife whose husband is all set to divorce her. She is sorry for her past behavior and wants to change to please him. At this point both parties are likely to suffer from the same problem: impatience. He will appreciate her efforts to improve but occasionally when out of habit she slips, he loses patience. He little realizes how difficult it is to change behavior that has become habitual over the years.

She too had better learn patience. When he loses his temper over her slips she could decide to yell at him because he still hasn't understood how much time she needs for change. Or she could decide gracefully to make allowance for his impatience. Major changes can occur quickly and can last, but they seldom do. Most of the time people take months and years to change and have many slips along the way.

He had been told to call home if he's going to be late for supper. He does this for two weeks and his wife is beginning to develop trust in him again. Then, one night he forgets and she doesn't see that any improvement has been made at all. Though it's possible for him never to goof up on that issue again, it just isn't likely. She needn't get distressed. If she puts the food away and goes out to a movie, he may get the message without a word having been said.

111

She'll be firm without being angry because she'll realize that no one is perfect, that regressions will happen, and that they're not the end of the world. Thus armed she'll be optimistic about the marriage and keep trying.

Another reason why it takes time to alter behavior is that new philosophies require time to be absorbed. If you have always believed that other people can upset you, just think what a radical change it is to accept the rational idea that you upset yourself. No one ever upsets you, you do it with your neurotic thinking. That's got to take time. Good counseling almost always requires the teaching of at least several new and startling ideas and seldom are these digested and accepted rapidly.

Give marriage counseling time to work for you. If you don't, you make it powerless.

4. The client fails to do homework assignments. Unless you do as the counselor suggests, counseling can't help you. If you are given an assignment to assert yourself against your spouse and week after week you stubbornly refuse to do your homework, you're not letting therapy help. You can talk in therapy about what you had better do, but until you do it the talk never converts to action.

Take the case of two lonely women. I urged both of them to overcome their shyness and be more aggressive in approaching men. Each had her eyes on a man she wanted to meet. The men did not make the overtures, so I advised each client to call up the gentleman in question and ask him to dinner. Both of them were uneasy at the prospect of rejection, of course. I argued that it was better to try and lose than not to try at all. Each had little to lose. They wouldn't be more lonely if the invitation was turned down and they just might win.

Ms. A. took a couple of jiggers of Scotch before making her call and was handsomely rewarded by the man gladly accepting. They were married several months later. Honestly!

Ms. B. simply would not put herself in a position to be rejected, so she refused. She left the office without making another appointment. You can bring clients to therapy but you can't make them better. Counseling is powerless if you refuse to work at the assignments that therapists frequently give.

Make the Effort

Enough said about divorce. This is a book on love and marriage and how to achieve success in both. I therefore want to close these pages with a statement on the desirability of becoming as mature as you can and learning to cope with neurotic habits in your mate which are only annoying, not harmful.

Many more marriages would survive quite satisfactorily if we simply did not let our mates disturb us. This means that we may have to put up with unreasonable behavior from time to time, but that need not be a cause of friction unless we allow it to be. To be the kind of mate who is easy to live with, we must conquer our natural tendency to make mountains out of molehills. I can't imagine anyone more difficult to live with (with the exception of seriously disturbed persons) than someone who is always overreacting.

How good it is to blunder and have your mate accept it graciously and without a long lecture. How pleasant it is to live with a spouse who wants your company but does not fall apart if you occasionally stay out too late. In these ways and many more you provide an emotional environment your partner will come to cherish. Your marriage has an upbeat quality when being around you is pleasant for your mate far more often than it is unpleasant. To keep it this way, you will want to keep your gripes down to a minimum. If you have a comment to make about your mate's behavior, make it in a positive way. Only when annoying behavior gets truly out of hand will you want to take firmer measures and raise a ruckus.

I suppose, if I had to give a brief description for a formula for success in marriage, I would put it this way: (1) Anger is the greatest enemy to a happy marriage. Be firm if you need be, but be polite, kind, and considerate while you are being firm. (2) Forgiveness and the acceptance of your mate as an imperfect human being is equally as important if love is to survive. No matter how much you love your spouse, time will soon enough reveal all manner of flaws. Accept most of them just as you want most of your own idiosyncrasies accepted.

If you will bear these two general rules in mind, I have every hope that your marriage will improve. But you must work at this task every bit as seriously as you work at your job. Marriage is a loving business and responds to most of the rules that govern business. Marriage, however, is a very special business. It is stronger and weaker, more pleasing and more frustrating, more enduring and more fragile, more blissful and more painful than any other relationship adults can enter.

May you live intimately and happily with the person of your choice to the end of your life.

Book List

To make the task of succeeding at marriage easier, let me refer you to books I have written that have proved helpful.

THE RATIONAL MANAGEMENT OF CHILDREN. 2d rev. ed. Libra Publishers, Inc., 1972.
Parents, teachers, and counselors will find easily understood explanations in this book on using the newest psychological insights concerning children's fears, depressions, and misbehaviors. Special emphasis has been placed on discipline and ways to control children without physical punishment.

REASON IN PASTORAL COUNSELING.
The Westminster Press, 1972.
Both the minister and the intelligent layman will learn about the new agreement between the teachings of religion and psychology. The pastoral counselor, in particular, will realize that many of today's newest psychological insights are extensions of age-old religious teachings. This book gives a number of verbatim case studies on the three major areas of neurotic behavior: anger, fear, and depression, and it shows the minister of every persuasion how he can counsel in a psychologically sophisticated manner without committing violence to his faith.

OVERCOMING DEPRESSION. The Westminster Press, 1973.
Here is a simple paperback, written for the person without formal training. Depression is treated as a condition caused by one or

more of the following three attitudes: self-blame, self-pity, and other-pity. The book then goes on to explain how each of these states can be changed, and the many case studies throughout make this task easier to understand.

OVERCOMING FRUSTRATION AND ANGER.
The Westminster Press, 1974.
It *is* possible to do something about that temper you have had all your life. You will learn that other people cannot anger you without your cooperation and you will also be taught what you must do to control your anger for months or years at a time.

OVERCOMING WORRY AND FEAR.
The Westminster Press, 1975.
Though it is impossible to eliminate worry and fear completely, we can control these emotions remarkably better if we follow certain suggestions. Making mountains out of molehills and focusing on our troubles are the two techniques to avoid if you wish to be more serene and less worried.

MARRIAGE AND THE MEMO METHOD, with Edmund S. Kean, M.D. The Westminster Press, 1975.
Communication is vital between two people in love. When talk no longer works, try writing. Memos, to be most effective, should be carefully organized and precise. The book tells how that can be done and offers other insights into how to get along with your mate.

HOW TO DO WHAT YOU WANT TO DO: THE ART OF SELF-DISCIPLINE. The Westminster Press, 1976.
One of the most important qualities to possess to use your talents to the fullest, to overcome dangerous habits (drinking, smoking, overeating), and to practice sound psychology to improve your health and marriage, is self-discipline which has been ignored for too long. This book can show you how to make you take command of yourself.